PRAISE FOR *LEAN OUT*

"Marissa's refreshing voice about systemic cognitive bias and the mental limitations holding women back—while supporting maleness—rings true with well-researched, commonsense insights that speak to the experiences of women in corporate America. Marissa is right about female traits like empathy, honesty, listening, and relationship competency being undervalued. Her candor and experiences in two tech-world giants are grounding, as they present scenarios and characters from across today's corporate environments.

Energized while reading *Lean Out*, I found myself repeatedly saying, 'YES, that's right!' Marissa is spot-on as she pulls the covers off how the game is played.

The ideas presented here for driving change are powerful, clear, and actionable. This book is a must read for insights on the impact that reversing systemic gender biases can have on creating more diverse, healthier workplaces for both women and men."

— Joanne Harell, Senior Director,
USA Citizenship, Microsoft

"For the first time in a long time, I finally read a book that states clear facts around the gender issues, with sound research backing the assumptions, in a simple way for men and women to comprehend. This book should be read by leaders of all types, as it provides a fresh perspective on valuing oneself without shame or blame, while preparing the reader for the corporate ladder."

— Dr. Betty Uribe, Executive Vice President, California
Bank & Trust and author of *#Values: The Secret
to Top Level Performance in Business and Life*

"*Lean Out* is a highly readable book that has 'leaned in' and listened to many—and maybe the majority of—women in the workplace. Many, many women will proclaim, 'Finally, an honest book that gets me, who I am, where I am, where I'm trying to get to, and the myriad of roadblocks stopping me.' If you're a working woman, read it to feel validated and less alone and uplifted in your struggle."

— Mark Goulston, author of *Just Listen: Discover the
Secret to Getting Through to Absolutely Anyone*

D1319573

"This book will make you think differently about what it will take for women to succeed in American business, by exploding myth after myth with cogent arguments and simple common sense."

"*Lean Out* spoke directly to my corporate experience. In fact, I left my tech career because I felt I couldn't be 'nice' and still get ahead. I wish I had the clarity I found in *Lean Out* earlier in my career. This book is a game changer and a must read for every young woman (and man) starting their career."

"Marissa Orr's *Lean Out* is the natural complement to Sheryl Sandberg's *Lean In*. Real, honest, and practical, Orr's wisdom empowers readers in both their career paths and personal lives to find significant meaning and well-being in all they do and achieve. No job may be great enough for the human spirit, but Orr reframes the perspective of success to alter our perception of what really matters. A brilliant addition to the library of talent development and diversity and inclusion and why twenty-first-century business can't survive without them."

LEAN OUT

THE TRUTH ABOUT WOMEN, POWER, AND THE WORKPLACE

MARISSA ORR

HarperCollins
LEADERSHIP

AN IMPRINT OF HarperCollins

Published by HarperCollins Leadership, an imprint of HarperCollins Focus LLC.

Any internet addresses, phone numbers, or company or product information printed in this book are offered as a resource and are not intended in any way to be or to imply an endorsement by HarperCollins Leadership, nor does HarperCollins Leadership vouch for the existence, content, or services of these sites, phone numbers, companies, or products beyond the life of this book.

ISBN 978-1-5955-5775-9 (eBook)
ISBN 978-1-5955-5756-8 (HC)
ISBN 978-1-4002-1604-8 (ITPE)

Library of Congress Control Number: 2019934279

Printed in the United States of America
HB 07.10.2019

For my parents, whose unconditional love has given me the courage to think for myself, out loud.

CONTENTS

CONTENTS

AUTHOR'S NOTE

This is a work of nonfiction. The events and experiences detailed are all true and have been faithfully rendered as I remember them, to the best of my ability. Though conversations come from my keen recollection of them, they are not written to represent word-for-word documentation; rather, I've retold them in a way that evokes what was said, in keeping with the nature and character of the events. I have also changed the names and identifying characteristics of my colleagues, as well as the names and features of the projects I worked on, in order to protect individuals' privacy and to avoid the possible disclosure of confidential information.

PROLOGUE

A Series of Fortunate Events

On a Sunday afternoon in March 2016, I hit Send on an email to Sheryl Sandberg, setting in motion a series of events that ended eighteen months later, when I was fired from my job at Facebook.

To explain, I first need to go back to the fall of 2014, which was my eleventh year working at Google. At the time, the company was organizing a spate of thought-leadership and training programs aimed at helping their female employees succeed. I've always been passionate about helping women, so naturally I got very involved in these efforts and attended everything Google offered on the topic. But after a while, I became disenchanted. The discussions never seemed to be real or honest, and they lacked any sort of practical application to our daily lives.

I decided to write my own perspective on the topic, and a month later, I was in a small conference room, delivering the presentation to a handful of women, most of whom were my close friends. Over time, however, more women showed up, and it grew from one presentation into a series of lectures I presented at other companies and even a few colleges across New York City. By the middle of 2015, I'd presented to more than a thousand people, and this little side project was bringing significant meaning into my life. And it was right around this time that I got the call from Facebook.

Until then, I'd never considered leaving Google. Although there were ups and downs, as with any job, for the most part I was happy, and my friends there were like family. But the more I talked to Facebook, the more it seemed like a perfect move. Less than half the size of Google, it was growing fast, with plenty of opportunities to work on exciting projects. And above all, this was the birthplace of *Lean In*. Would anywhere else on earth be more likely to support my work on the women's leadership series?

As a single mom of three kids, I did have a lot of important things to consider before making such a big change. Being rash and impulsive, I disregarded most of them. This was Facebook. Obviously, they would understand and support my need for flexibility. Besides, nothing was going to crush my fangirl dreams of being discovered by Sheryl Sandberg, who, blown away by my brilliance and passion for helping women, would give me a one-way ticket out of my day job. I started at Facebook in February 2016, eager, optimistic, and blissfully unaware of the downward spiral in which I was about to step.

Sheryl Sandberg and I are from the same hometown: a small Jewish community in an unincorporated part of Dade County, Florida, about halfway between South Beach and Fort Lauderdale. We went to the same grade schools and grew up in homes less than half a mile apart. The parallels continued into adulthood, as we joined Google in its halcyon days before they went public, pursued our mutual passion for helping women, and now both worked at Facebook.

For all the things we had in common, there were just as many we did not. The most obvious being that she was a billionaire and the COO of one of the world's largest corporations, and I was nowhere close to being either of those things. There were also the minor details: she had two Harvard degrees, launched Google.org, served as chief of staff for the United States secretary of the Treasury, founded LeanIn.org, served on the boards of Disney and Starbucks, was named one of *Time*'s most influential people, and was designated *Forbes*'s fifth most powerful woman in business. I, on the other hand, went to the University of Florida, where my biggest accomplishment upon graduating was not having died of alcohol poisoning.

Despite the childhood and career connections, Sandberg had no idea who I was. We were ten years apart in school, and she was ten layers above me at Google, so we'd never met. Over the years, I thought about reaching out to her to introduce myself but could never muster the courage, and I wasn't quite sure what I'd say anyway.

My first week at Facebook, however, I found out she'd be speaking onstage at our sales conference the following week in San Francisco. Figuring this was the perfect opportunity to reach out, I drafted an email introducing myself, and asked if she could spare a minute to meet in person. After writing and rewriting the email at least a hundred times, I nervously hit Send. And a couple of hours later, when she replied with a gracious offer to meet for twenty minutes before she took the stage at the conference, I was elated.

The next week I found myself waiting outside the stage area for Sandberg's assistant, Paige, ten minutes before we were scheduled to meet. Trying to be cool and casual, but failing miserably, I fidgeted with the hem of my dress and silently recited Stuart Smalley affirmations about being good enough and smart enough. Paige finally showed up and led me through a maze of hallways to the greenroom. When we arrived, Sandberg turned to me and smiled. I remember thinking she was much smaller than I'd expected. I mean, I wasn't necessarily picturing Hulk Hogan in a dress, but I guess I just assumed she'd be more physically imposing. But she was petite, and I felt like a bumbling, awkward giant. Then, I made it way worse: I went in for a hug. I know. *I know.* And it was just as bad as you might expect—the half-second embrace was weird and cold, and I felt as though I'd violated her before we even sat down.

She pointed to a couple of steel folding chairs, and we sat across from each other as she asked a couple of questions about my time at Facebook thus far. Still recovering from the hug, I pretended to be cool and in control, while she pretended to be interested in what I was saying. Grasping for some kind of human connection, I dropped a few names of people we knew from back home, trying to spark more gossipy-girlfriend type of conversation. This, too, went as badly as you might expect, as things were only getting more awkward. I was about to give up when the subject changed, and she made a passing reference to the career challenges of single moms. Ah, something real! I snapped back into my normal self and, for the next few minutes, rambled on about the hard times in my life and what they taught me about perseverance and confidence and self-respect.

As I continued, she leaned toward me, her eyes widening and head nodding.

Wait. Could it be . . . ? I think . . . I think she's into me.

Feeling emboldened, I continued on about being grateful for the hard times in life because they made me feel as if I could do anything (except get promoted, but we'll get to that later on). As I became more myself, she seemed to get more real, too, and at one point stopped me midsentence.

"Do you mind if I get my laptop for a second? Sorry, but this is really powerful stuff, and I just want to write it down."

Um, what? This could not be for real. But it was, and for the rest of the meeting, Sheryl Sandberg went on to *transcribe* everything I was saying. *OMG, she really does care about what I have to say!* Well, sort of.

"I have to get onstage now, but listen—I'm writing a book on resilience and think you and your story would make a perfect feature. Do you mind if my researcher emails you to set up an interview and discuss next steps?"

"That would be great! Thank you, Sheryl!" Clearly, we were going to be besties now; first names seemed appropriate.

I was on cloud nine. Just seven days at Facebook, and I had impressed Sheryl Sandberg. I fantasized about all the brilliant things I was going to contribute to her book, how she'd recognize my potential and pluck me from corporate obscurity.

After the conference I returned to New York and plunged myself into the new job. I hadn't heard back from Sandberg or her book researcher, so I put it out of my mind and focused on work. Things went smoothly for about two weeks, when suddenly, I became a victim of workplace bias. I don't mean bias toward men, but toward those in power. More specifically, toward the whims of a powerful female executive named Kimberly, who, for a reason I couldn't quite discern, was silently enraged that I existed.

My third week on the job, we had our first meeting together, just the two of us. Up to that point, I had held Kimberly in the highest regard. She had also worked at Google, and although I didn't know her directly, she had a tremendous reputation and was well-liked by almost everyone.

Kimberly was also the person who'd finally convinced me to join Facebook. During the recruitment process, she had showered me with outlandish compliments and knew exactly what to say to make me feel like . . . she gets me. Her enthusiasm and flattery were so over the top they bordered on cartoonish, but all my ego could see was validation and the promise of accolades on the horizon. At one point, I did hear a small voice in my head whisper, *She doesn't even know you*, which in retrospect was a big, flashing red warning sign sent from my subconscious. But my ego persisted, *She must have heard about how great I am from George*, a mutual friend who now worked for her. So humble of me.

I approached Kimberly outside the conference room for our meeting, and right away I sensed that her attitude toward me had changed. As the door clicked shut behind us, the fake, perfunctory smile vanished from her lips, and a look of icy annoyance flashed across her face. Outside that door, where the world was watching, she was one person. Sitting across from me, where I was the only witness, she had transformed into someone entirely different.

It reminded me of Large Marge from *Pee-wee's Big Adventure*. That scene haunted me as a child. The image of her human mask being ripped off and her eyeballs shooting out like yo-yos from alien-like sockets. I understood Pee-wee's terror as he watched her transformation. Some of the scariest moments in life are when we find out we're not dealing with the person we thought we were.

I'll never forget the smug look of anticipation on Kimberly's face as we sat down. Whatever she was about to say, she was going to enjoy it.

"Marissa, I'm going to give you a little bit of feedback."

Hmm. That was odd, considering I'd worked there for a hot minute and still didn't know how to use Outlook. But sure, I'm always open to feedback!

"We hired you because we know you're good. So, you don't have to go around trying to prove it to everyone. You're coming off as frazzled and out of control."

The gut punches kept coming. I ask too many questions. I'm never happy. I'm trying too hard. I spoke up just once during all of this, to ask, "Are there specific examples you can share that would help me understand why I'm appearing this way?"

She paused, started to go in one direction, then seemed to change her mind. With a dismissive brush of her hand, she answered, "Look, Marissa, you're just not the same person you were in the interview process."

Funny, I was just thinking the same thing about you! But okay. I got what this was now. After the tongue-lashing, we walked out of the conference room together, and her persona of lovely, benevolent leader returned. Just in time for her to be seen by anyone who actually mattered.

The following months were a blur. I was supposed to be Kimberly's marketing and strategy partner, but her apparent disdain for me made this impossible. Not about to let a pesky thing like my *humanity* get in the way, she refused to acknowledge my existence or engage me directly. She didn't reply to my emails and deleted all of our meetings from the calendar, so I found it almost impossible to do my job, or to do anything, really. The problem was compounded by the fact that I was brand-new and didn't know anybody yet. Kimberly, on the other hand, had a sterling reputation and had been at Facebook for over three years. I tried talking to my manager about what was happening, but she only knew Kimberly's perky, public mask. She assumed we were dealing with a normal situation that could easily be solved with mature, grown-up communication.

My attempts to explain what was happening only made me look bad. "She won't talk to meeeee!" doesn't come off the same way in the office as it does in the schoolyard. I would start to tell someone, then stop when I heard how petty and immature it made me sound. Panicked about not being able to do my job and not having anyone to confide in about it, I started feeling isolated and depressed.

One night I went out to dinner with a few of my former Google coworkers. When they asked how things were going at Facebook, I danced around the subject a bit. But as soon as I mentioned Kimberly, my friend Jocelyn interrupted.

"Wait—you're working with Kimberly? Okay, I know what this is about."

Jocelyn had spent several years working for Kimberly, and for the majority of that time, things were great. But one day, everything suddenly crumbled. She explained:

"I passed by Donna [Kimberly's boss] in the café one day, and she asked how things were going on our team. I suspected Kimberly didn't like it when we talked to people above her, but what was I going to do? Not say anything? Anyway, Donna invited me to sit down with her, and we ended up having a really great conversation over lunch. I never said anything about Kimberly—her name didn't even come up! But it doesn't matter. Kimberly hates that shit."

You know those pictures that were popular in the '90s, the ones that looked like a random bunch of colors and lines, but then suddenly, if you looked at it right, a 3-D picture emerged? A second ago it looked like an abstract mess, but now you can see the picture so clearly. That's what it was like after hearing Jocelyn's story. Everything snapped together, and I could make sense of why Kimberly's attitude might have taken such a swift and vicious turn only three weeks into my job. She was probably pissed about my meeting with Sandberg. I had seen the two women scooting around together occasionally, but it never occurred to me that my meeting with her would be seen as some sort of political maneuver. I mean, I went in hoping to gossip like old friends! But it was clear that Kimberly probably saw it as a power move and a threat to their budding courtship.

From that angle, I could only imagine what she was thinking when I told her how well my meeting went: *Who the hell does this girl think she is, meeting with Sheryl in her second week, when I've had to kiss her ass for three years?*

The absurdity of it all was almost amusing, and I felt better now that I could make sense of things. But it didn't change the situation. And in fact, things were only getting worse.

Six months into my time at Facebook, I got a call from human resources (HR). Someone—I still don't know who—had told our HR business partner that she or he suspected Kimberly was bullying me, and it was Facebook's policy to investigate any and all claims of that nature.

Kimberly was a powerful executive with friends in high places; there was no way this could turn out well for me. But declining to pursue the matter wasn't an option; my participation was required. To address my concerns, the HR rep gave me a rundown of Facebook's anti-retaliation policy, emphasizing that I would not be punished for speaking the truth. I thought about all the people who'd heard that line right before they ended up dead.

I was panicked at first and tried to come up with a strategy. Picturing myself as Bobby Axelrod in the Showtime series *Billions*, I imagined the investigation as a chess game, plotting out my next moves. Then I remembered that I possess neither political savvy nor the ability to keep words inside my brain, which meant there was a 99.9 percent chance I was going to tell them every single honest-to-God detail.

I accepted my fate and surrendered to the situation. At one point, I even became a little excited by the drama of it all. You know how on *Sex and the City*, the girls would meet for brunch and share the gory details of all the messed-up things men had done to them? And how they'd laugh at the ridiculousness, reminding each other that they're amazing women who deserve better? Yeah, well that's what I imagined my meetings with HR would be like during the investigation. I know. *I know.*

The investigation concluded eight weeks later, and surprise! It was nothing like my fantasy, and everything like the reality that a sane person would have expected: no evidence of bullying was found.

Two months after the investigation concluded, and only eight months into my time at Facebook, I got the news that I was being put on a performance improvement plan, or PIP for short. PIPs are supposed to help failing employees improve their job performance. But in reality, getting put on one means the company is planning to fire you, and the PIP covers their ass from a legal perspective. My identity as a conscientious, well-respected hard worker was completely unraveled.

The official PIP document included my impending termination date and the key reasons for my poor performance, the biggest of which was my failure to build good relationships with Kimberly and her team. I was incredulous.

I called June, our new HR business partner, and asked how one might go about developing a good relationship with someone who was just investigated for bullying you. That was when I learned that June had no idea about the investigation. She had joined shortly after it concluded, and nobody had filled her in. I summarized what had happened and mentioned the anti-retaliation policy that was supposedly going to protect me from this exact situation. She said to give her some time to learn more about all of this, and she'd follow up with me in the coming weeks.

June was no dummy. She was a seasoned HR professional who knew this was a ridiculous situation and that someone had obviously screwed up. The legal implications were crystal clear. Now she needed time to figure out how to fix it and keep Facebook out of trouble.

My performance made a miraculous recovery after talking to June, and like magic, I was off the PIP. I was relieved, but in the back of my mind, I knew I was a dead man walking.

Everyone around me, both at work and in my personal life, encouraged me to leave and find a new job elsewhere. But I'd already decided to ride out the remainder of the year at Facebook and then return to working on my women's leadership series. The course of events forced me to come to terms with what I'd always known but until then refused to admit: I was never going to be truly happy in the corporate world. In my heart, I desperately wanted to pursue my dream of writing a book and being a public speaker. So, I chose to see the time at Facebook as a gift, a chance to maintain an income while I figured out a plan to pursue things that mattered.

One of the first things I did was reread *Lean In* as a starting point for my research. The first time I read it was in 2014, when I'd just begun working on my lecture series. With the excitement and novelty of a new project as the backdrop, I enjoyed the book and admired Sandberg's courage.

But now I was reading it through an entirely different lens, and it led me to a significant realization: *Lean In* was completely antithetical to everything I taught in my workshops and ran counter to everything I believe as a human being. *Lean In* is a battle cry for women to change—to be more assertive, ambitious, and demanding. In other words, it pins the blame for the gender gap squarely on women and offers a prescription on how to behave more like men. I, on the other hand, blamed the failure of our institutions, which haven't changed since the industrial age, a time when few women were in the workforce. I encouraged women to reject the dogma and rhetoric about what they should want and who they're supposed to be, and offered a framework for defining success purely on their terms. The entire spirit of my lectures was irreverent and tinged with a subtle corporate rebelliousness.

I don't know why the contrast between our approaches was so invisible to me the first time around. But when I read Sandberg's book the second time, the profound irony hit me with a sharp smack to the face. When it came to success, I had been listening to her advice instead of my own. And I was angry. Angry at myself for buying into someone else's idea of who I should be and what my career should look like. Angry because none of it was real, and angry because, deep down, I had known it all along.

That summer I was sitting in an audience at a women's leadership breakfast when Sheryl Sandberg took the stage with none other than Kimberly. They both sat down and began a discussion about female empowerment in the workplace. Kimberly told the audience all the things she does to support the women around her, always going the extra mile to help women succeed. This seemed to please Sandberg, and the audience politely clapped while I tried not to throw up. I wanted to scream, "None of this is real! This isn't even about women! It's about power and personal agenda." How could I not have seen this all along?

In that moment, I made a promise to myself. Instead of getting angry and self-righteous about the theater of feminism, I would continue sharing my truth and telling my story.

Despite making significant progress on my own book several months after the conference, I was still too terrified to straight-up quit my job. Thankfully, the universe stepped in and did it for me. By "universe," I mean a call from June on my way home from what I thought was a regular day at the office. She said that despite my marginal improvements, I still wasn't meeting the expectations for someone at my level. And with that, I was fired.

Oh, and the anti-retaliation policy? Its protection only lasts so long, and my time had just run out.

———

This prologue is meant to give you a sense of who I am and why I wrote this book. But *Lean Out* isn't about Sheryl Sandberg or my time at

Facebook. Rather, it's about unraveling the larger dogma and rhetoric currently dominating the national conversation on women and work. My experiences at Facebook and Google are only recounted to support the larger arguments outlined in the following pages.

Feminism isn't about making women stronger. Women are already strong. It's about changing the way the world perceives that strength.

—G. D. ANDERSON

INTRODUCTION

First, we know we're not crazy, the system is crazy.

—GLORIA STEINEM

Lean Out is a book based on my original lecture series that I started at Google over five years ago. As previously mentioned, I started the project after becoming disenchanted with Google's various programs that were supposedly empowering women. But I couldn't connect the dots on how any of it would help us succeed.

Perhaps the most difficult part for me to accept was the incessant stream of advice on how to behave. Instead of encouraging us to lean into our individual strengths and celebrate the value women bring to the table, we were essentially being told to behave more like men. Of course, nobody said it like that. This was the corporate world. Instead, they called it "success behaviors," which really meant "male behaviors," but changing the word made everyone feel better. Is there anything *less* feminist than implying that men are the "norm" and they're doing it "right," and that there's something inherently less valuable about the way we are as women?

My disenchantment slowly gained strength, and the final straw, the one that originally inspired my lecture series, happened during a women's workshop on "successful communication" at Google, which I attended with my best friend, Carol.

I'd met Carol ten years earlier, when we shared an office shortly after she joined Google, and she is now more like a sister to me than a friend. And yet, despite ten years of deep friendship, I still occasionally bristle at her aloof tone and the directness with which she communicates. For example, when we arrange a girls' night out, our text conversation usually goes something like this:

Me: Cannnnnot wait to catch up over drinks tonight! Need margarita stat 🍸🍸🍸‼️💟🍷🍸🍷🍹 xoxoxo

Carol: k

Me: *<Feels pang of anxiety.>*

   <Wonders if she's mad at me.>

   <Takes mental inventory of what I could have possibly done wrong.>

   <Scrolls through calendar to see if I missed her daughter's birthday.>

   <Checks email to make sure I responded to anything important.>

   <Debates whether to be annoying and ask her if she's mad.>

   <Knows I will do this anyway because I'm neurotic and obsessive.>

Me: Is everything okay?

Carol: Yes. Restaurant gets busy so pls don't be late.

Me: *<Decides she's definitely mad.>*

    <Knows I can't ask her again because I'm already annoying as hell.>

    <Decides I will get there early and have a drink before she arrives.>

    <Tries to let it go.>

    <Can't let it go.>

Me: 😣

    <Sends emoji with ambiguous expression to communicate that I'm uncertain of how she's feeling toward me and that she should throw me a bone, an emoji, something, *to make me feel better.>*

Carol: <no response>

Me: *<Gives up.>*

    <Makes note to talk to therapist about my anxiety.>

    <Googles "generalized anxiety disorder.">

    <Gets anxious from reading the results.>

    <Puts phone away and goes back to work.>

    <Remembers I hate work and leave early for a drink.>

It's not a stretch to say Carol and I communicate differently. She's direct, to the point, and wouldn't be caught dead using an emoji. I'm more expressive, and you've gotten the point about my relationship to emojis. Like most things in life, each communication style has its good and its bad.

Or not. According to the communication workshop we were

attending, mine was just bad. Over the two-day course, we learned all the ways women undermine themselves, and how to behave more assertively. We learned that women apologize more often than men, speak more emotionally, and use qualifiers such as "I might be wrong, but," or "I'm no expert, but." As the instructor lambasted us for our shameful use of exclamation points and our expressions of icky girl things, like feelings, I turned to Carol and whispered, "You can leave now." It was clear the instructor's advice wasn't aimed at her; she had a black belt in this shit already.

During the next section of the course, we learned that men are more likely to state their views as facts, even when they're unsure it's a fact. They communicate with the intention to establish authority (even when they don't have said authority) and often don't take the perspective or concern of the listener into account. Shocking, right? I mean, tell us something we don't know!

Then, our instructor told us something we didn't know: their bravado and self-aggrandizement are precisely what make men more successful at work. So, if we wanted to be just as successful, we needed to be arrogant too.

Carol sat on one side of me, and on the opposite side of me sat our former manager, Kathy. Kathy was a walking example of someone who communicates with certainty and with the intent to ~~crush your dreams~~ establish authority. Her self-centered arrogance was obvious to everyone except those above her in the food chain. Despite our team being tortured for the duration of her eighteen-month reign, she had just been promoted to the coveted title of senior director. Her natural talent for ~~being an asshole~~ speaking with authority seemed to prove our instructor's point: the more assertive, the better, because nice girls don't succeed.

During the two-day workshop, there was no discussion on any

positive aspects of what I suppose is a "female" style of communication. It was as if we were better off not even admitting we spoke like *girls*. It felt like shame. Like, don't be so *you*, or you'll never succeed. It was disappointing, but I was starting to understand it.

Having studied influence and communication over a decade, I knew that the most effective styles have a balance of authority *and* warmth. In fact, research has shown that listening, empathy, and emotional intelligence are more important than directness when it comes to being influential and effective.[1] They are traits correlated more highly among women.[2] So why weren't we teaching *men* to speak more like *us*? Because these traits, while valuable in the real world, don't translate the same way inside the unique power dynamics of a large corporation. A corporate hierarchy has a specific, unspoken set of rules for winning. One of the biggest: pretending to know everything will get you way further than actually knowing anything. Thank God there are men around to show us how it's done!

The workshop I attended with Carol was the turning point that inspired me to write my own thought-leadership perspective for women at the company. I was trying to get across two main points. The first was that the prescriptions for female success hinged on us being more like men, which carried the implication that women are inferior. This was not only insulting but also wrongheaded. My second point was that the gender gap wasn't caused by dysfunctional women, which almost everyone seemed to be implying, but by a severely dysfunctional system.

A competitive hierarchy is simply a construct, developed by men in the industrial age, to organize and motivate other men, since few women were in the labor force at the time. It also originated in an era when most employees produced actual things, for example, assembling parts or building trains or whatever it is people do with things like steel. Employee performance was visible and objective and could be compared easily. Johnny clocked in, pumped out five cars, and clocked out.

Today, of course, the economy is radically different, and output is mostly delivered in the form of intellect, critical thinking, creativity, and imagination—things you can't see, which makes it harder to tell who's doing a good job. In this ambiguity, and without objective means of measuring output, our brains default to what's most visible—like aggression, self-promotion, and self-aggrandizement—using these proxies to determine who's winning. These proxies may correlate more highly with men than with women, but they don't correlate with competence.

We're at an incredibly sharp inflection point. Our systems of organizing employees, evaluating performance, and motivating people were built by men, from a male worldview, with the intention of making their male employees more productive. They were built to serve an economy that's long gone. While the whole world, the entire fabric of our economy, and the composition of our workforce have transformed since then, our systems have remained almost exactly the same. The dysfunction also suffocates creativity and innovation and reduces well-being among the country's workforce.

To close the gender gap, what makes more sense: rewiring women's personalities or rewiring the system to better meet their needs?

Problems can be solved only when the root cause is well understood. Therefore, it's critical to examine and test our understanding of why the gender gap exists. But we've mostly jumped straight to solutions, without a deep examination into why the problem exists in the first place. We've accepted the reasons we've been given and, as we'll explore later, have been scared to ask why or offer any dissenting opinion. But we must. We must question and poke and prod and examine and inspect—the stakes are too high not to. Without shining a light on where we've gone wrong, there's no hope for getting it right and little chance for real progress.

Part I of the book unravels the major tenets of conventional wisdom on women at work. Chapter 1 explains how we got to this point and why today's feminist leaders have failed to make progress. Chapters 2–6 each debunk a different theory behind the gender gap and the related elements of modern feminism. Part II, chapters 7 and 8, stitches things back together and presents a new model of understanding about what causes the gender gap. Part III, chapters 9 and 10, offers a new way forward for women individually and corporate America at large.

A few important caveats: in different chapters I make the point that, generally speaking, there are significant differences in personality and behavior across men and women, and that these differences aren't just a product of culture; they also have a biological component. As such, absolutely *nothing* in this book, in any way, shape, or form, can be used to explain or argue *anything* related to racial, religious, and ethnic diversity, or affirmative action. Ethnicity and gender are two totally different, unrelated things, and cannot be lumped together when it comes to diversity. For example, men and women have different physical organs that produce different levels of certain hormones. Obviously, the same cannot be said when comparing whites and blacks, Hispanics and Asians, Jews and Catholics, and so on. The lack of female CEOs and the lack of black CEOs are born from two distinct and unrelated systemic issues. The latter has to do with socioeconomic, historical, and cultural forces that are outside the scope of this book.

The second caveat is that the arguments I make about the gender gap are specific to corporate America. Although the corporate gender gap may share similarities with gender diversity issues in other realms, such as politics and small business, it isn't exactly analogous, and therefore outside the scope of this book.

Finally, I recognize that in many ways, what I address in the following chapters are very much "first world problems." At times I feel silly even making arguments around what's best for an elite set of professional women, when far more pressing concerns face this nation's women. But in the end, this is part of my whole point. We've wasted a tremendous amount of time and resources without making substantial progress. By recognizing where we've gone wrong, we can direct our time, money, and attention toward solving problems that will make the greatest impact on the largest number of women.

PART ONE

ONE

SILENCING THE LAMBS

It's hard to go against the beliefs of powerful people. Therefore, for each of us, as difficult as it may be to accept, reality has a lot to do with what a lot of us or some important or powerful people say it is.

—William Glasser, MD, *Choice Theory*

"Raise your hand if you were called bossy growing up."

This was the first thing Sheryl Sandberg said as she took the stage in front of two hundred women at a female leadership breakfast in Detroit. Her comment wasn't delivered with the curious tone you'd expect from someone genuinely interested in the answer. Rather, it was said with an expectant nod and knowing look, as if she were really saying, "I know you hated being called bossy as much as I did, so raise your freaking hand!" Which is ironic because she was being kinda bossy about it.

Slumped in the seat next to me, my friend Jackie half-heartedly raised her hand. Knowing for certain she'd never been called bossy a day in her life, I turned to her and rolled my eyes. With a look of confusion, she crouched down low, cupped her hand over her mouth, and whispered, "What? What did she even say? I wasn't listening."

Sandberg went on to make the point that women are punished for being assertive at work. They are accused of being bossy or too pushy, whereas men who assert themselves are seen as leaders. As a result, we mute ourselves, lower our ambition, and give men the advantage.

Jackie's chronic lack of assertiveness at work could easily be seen as evidence of Sandberg's point. But it wasn't, because it was due to something much simpler than social conditioning. Like so many of us, Jackie didn't *care* enough about her job to be demanding about it.

After the day of empowering lectures on how to be ~~more like men~~ your best self, Jackie and I went out for margaritas. As we plopped ourselves down on a couple of barstools, I asked her why Sandberg talked about bossiness so much.

"Because she's bossy. And she probably gets a lot of shit for it."

"I get that, but I don't know many other women who struggle with that kind of thing. Why do we always talk about it so much at these women's events?"

"Because bossy people are in charge of them."

Oh, right.

During countless conversations with my girlfriends over the years, we complained about almost everything. Being ashamed of our bossiness was perhaps #827 on the list. You know what was way higher? Being bullied by senior women who felt threatened by other females. That was something I never heard discussed openly, even though it was such a central challenge for many of us. Just bring up the subject among professional female friends, and the conversation can last until the third glass of wine. (We'll get to this in more detail later—the secret bullying, not the secret alcoholism.) Number 4 on the list: we were already the CEOs of our households and often felt unappreciated for our efforts, so we were ambivalent about seeking promotions; it seemed like *more* responsibility for even *less* acknowledgment.

At Google and Facebook, the gender gap was a hot topic, with a lot of involvement from senior leaders. But across their dozens of women's leadership events over the years, we rarely addressed any of these important issues. Because the events were high-profile, they were co-opted by opportunists who sounded more like corporate cheerleaders giving hollow stump speeches than like people who were interested in solving a real problem. Most women's initiatives devolved into platforms for visibility and a means to advance one's career rather than serve as real change agents. This is perhaps why, despite my strong feminist leanings, I could never identify with the leaders who took the stage on women's issues. And I don't think many other women in the audience did either.

I often wondered what would happen if, instead of the parade of powerful women, a lower-level manager juggling a household, kids, a husband, and a personal life took the mic and said, "Raise your hand if you're apathetic about your job because it's all politics and bullshit anyway." Would the majority of us once again have our hands in the air? Perhaps. We can't know for sure because nobody ordinary appears onstage, and it's a question no one ever asks.

The lack of authenticity wasn't isolated to public conversations on female empowerment. It also governed the politics of our individual careers. As I discovered right away, the first rule of being a woman at work is to never tell the truth about all the reasonable feelings and concerns you have about being a woman at work. I've always been bad at knowing what I can and can't say in certain situations, so I learned this painful lesson early and often.

5

One such time at Google, I had been in the same job for too long and was itching for a new role at the company. I found one I really wanted and quickly scored an interview with the hiring manager, Elizabeth. Since I came highly recommended by mutual colleagues, and she wouldn't have to spend time training someone new, I figured I was a shoo-in.

Ten minutes into our interview, however, I started to sweat. Cool and confident walking in, I was now fumbling my way through even the softball questions. Elizabeth graduated cum laude from Oxford and had an MBA from Wharton. A former star in the consulting world, she'd trotted the globe telling CEOs how to run their billion-dollar organizations. And all the while, she built a side business that helped fund local charities in New York.

This would have been intimidating enough, but what made it worse was her restless energy, endless fidgeting, and frenetic pace of speech. Her brain processed my answers faster than I could talk. I'd barely eke out a sentence before she'd nod vigorously, raise her hand, and signal me to stop.

"I'd say my strengths are in the realm of creativity, since I—"

"Yep. Got it. Makes sense. Okay. Next . . ."

I sank farther down in my chair with each new question.

"How do you define advancement or your career goals overall?"

I gave my standard answer, one I'd given a hundred times before during performance reviews and career planning conversations.

"I don't really see it as a vertical-type ladder, like most people . . ."

I paused, giving her the chance to understand my point before I made it. But she was quiet, so I continued.

". . . I see it as circles of impact. Contributing more to the business or helping more and more people is my signpost for growth and advancement. It's more rewarding than a promotion."

For the first time since the interview began, Elizabeth sat back and smiled. Obviously, she was impressed with my use of the word *signpost*.

"Marissa, I really love that. I really do—that's such a great way to think about it."

I felt about five inches taller.

But it didn't last, and for the remaining questions we went back to our initial dynamic of brilliant prodigy frustrated by bumbling moron. When it ended, I returned to my desk and told my good friend Greg how badly I had blown it. To salvage any remnants of self-respect, I mentioned the one bright spot.

"There was one thing I said that she actually liked . . ." I went on to tell him about my answer on career advancement.

"Oh my God. You are an idiot. *Who says that?*"

I was incredulous.

"What do you mean? She *loved* it! It was the only thing I said that didn't make her wonder how the hell I got a job here in the first place!"

Now Greg was incredulous.

"*Of course* she loved it. It means you're someone she can throw more and more work on without the bother of having to fight for your promotion. You basically just gave her carte blanche to shit all over you."

"Oh my God."

"She's gonna hire you. Watch—I guarantee it. Then you're really screwed."

"F*ck."

The truth was, I *didn't* care about being promoted. The only things that mattered to me were money and compliments. As long as those two things were in ample supply, I was happy. But everyone else seemed to care about promotions so much, I doubted my instincts and figured I was being dumb or naive. Or worse. Maybe I was committing the gravest of female professional sins: doubting my ambition. (Gasp!)

7

I did get the job on Elizabeth's team, and in the years following the spectacular failure of political savvy, I dropped the martyr stuff and tried playing the game on its own terms. I was doing a great job of keeping up the facade and advancing at a decent clip. Everything was going so well that sometimes I even forgot I was acting! My delusional world was a safe, happy place. But like most acts, it eventually ended.

The curtain on my days of deluded ambition closed during a two-year span in which I birthed three children, went through a traumatic divorce, singlehandedly moved the four of us to a new town, and began a new life as a single, working mom.

People say women lean out of their careers when they have kids, so they can spend more time with them, or for financial reasons or because of childcare issues. All are absolutely true. But I also think there's another reason. With their time squeezed and their energy scarce, women have a dramatically lower tolerance for politics, power games, and office bullshit.

After the birth of my twins (my older son was only two at the time), I tried figuring out how to handle the magnitude of work to do at home without compromising a promotion I was on track to receive and that was the culmination of many years of hard work. I didn't care about the title change, and I wasn't thrilled about the added responsibility, but I wanted the salary increase. Now that I was running a day care at home while fulfilling the demands of my day job, I was afraid of losing the raise. In a meeting with my manager, Dana, I asked what I'd need to do to stay on track.

Dana said she was planning to submit my promotion after the next review cycle, and that to get it approved, I'd need to start managing people. The peers on my team—the same level as me and all reporting to Dana—each managed at least five people, whereas I had no direct reports. I've always preferred to do work instead of lording over others who do the work, so I'd made the conscious choice to be an individual contributor instead of a manager. But as Dana explained, Google's policy prevented me from getting a promotion without having direct reports. The fact that I had the highest scores on our team made no difference. It was a hard-and-fast rule that beyond my level, you were required to manage people.

My valiant effort to hold back a fountain of tears lasted precisely no seconds.

"Dana, of course I want to be promoted. But I also wanna do *work*. Managing a team means I won't be able to get deep into projects or be creative. And frankly, I'm a single mom of three *babies*. I'm responsible for enough people at home; I don't want to be responsible for people at work. I just wanna *do* work."[1]

It was the only time I was ever direct and honest with a manager about my resistance to being promoted and advancing my career. Although this resistance was likely interpreted as a lack of ambition, it wasn't. I did have a desire to do interesting work. I wanted to solve problems and make an impact on the business. But managing a team wouldn't help me do that. My time would be spent managing other people's work and creating endless PowerPoints to explain to the higher-ups what it was we did at work all day, since most of them had no clue what was going on in their own departments.

Alas, these weren't the kinds of things people at Google said out loud, lest they ruin their chances to "succeed."

At Google, if you're at the same level for too many years without getting promoted, you're in danger of being put on a path toward the exit door. It doesn't matter how amazing you are at your job, and how much world-changing work you're doing. If you haven't been promoted in five years or more, HR starts breathing down your neck. *Why* you haven't been promoted, whether it's a personal choice or not, doesn't matter.[2] As a result, people go for promotions even when they don't want them, just to save their asses.

Indifference toward climbing the corporate ladder is treated universally as a negative. The entire goal of women's leadership seminars and training programs is to help you advance along with your male peers. Voicing reluctance is tantamount to exposing some secret failing and is a betrayal to our identities as modern, empowered women. As a result, there's a distinct lack of honesty in the public conversation about women at work. Dominated by a singular chorus of voices, we focus on tangential things, like bossiness, instead of addressing more significant issues that affect a larger portion of women. If we aren't honest about what's *actually* going on, how can we ever fix it?

PERSPECTIVE-BLIND MAN

An ancient Indian parable called "The Blind Men and the Elephant" loosely goes as follows:

A group of blind men heard that a strange animal called an elephant had been brought to the town, but none of them were aware of its shape and form. Curious, they said, "We must inspect and know it by touch, of which we are capable." So, they sought it out, and when they found it, they groped about it. The first man, whose hand landed on the elephant's trunk, said, "This being is like a thick snake." To another, whose hand reached the elephant's ear, it seemed like a kind of fan. The third man, whose hand was on the elephant's leg, said, "The elephant is a pillar, like a tree trunk." The blind man who placed his hand upon the elephant's side said, "The elephant is a wall." Another, who felt the elephant's tail, described the elephant as a rope. The last man felt its tusk, stating that the elephant was hard and smooth, like a spear.

The story has several different endings. In one version, the blind men discover that they all see the elephant as something very different. Each man believes the others are being dishonest, and the group devolves into violent conflict. Another version ends with the men listening to each other's perspectives, considering all points of view, and therefore seeing the whole elephant. In a third version, a sighted man enters the scene and describes each person's perspective to the group; the men learn they were right about the elephant from their individual perspectives, but wrong from the others'.

Using the elephant as a metaphor for society's understanding of the gender gap, it has been defined by those who see only its trunk. Its causes and solutions have been established by a handful of powerful and elite women who have broken the glass ceiling and whose voices have dominated the public discourse. They all appear to agree on the biggest challenges women face at work and offer the same kinds of advice. Mostly reflecting their individual experiences, the narrative falls along these lines: they were afraid to speak up; they were punished for being bossy or assertive; they navigated work-life balance; they practiced confidence; they defied cultural pressures; and so on.

The homogeneity of the narrative wouldn't necessarily be a problem if other voices were in the mix. But no mainstream books are written by women who are still looking up at the glass ceiling from way down below. We conduct research and polls to capture the spirit of their challenges, but their perspectives aren't represented in the mainstream conversations.

There is some logic to this. If we're trying to get more women to the top of the ladder, shouldn't the authorities be the ones who are there already? What can we possibly learn about the gender gap from a corporate dropout, like me? Am I not the cautionary tale we're trying to avoid?

To take a page from the progressive ethos of Silicon Valley, failure is the best way to learn. In solving problems, failure is far more valuable than success because it shines a light on what's broken. The perspectives of those who've failed to break the glass ceiling have the potential to illuminate where we've gone wrong, and sometimes a new perspective is all it takes to make a leap of progress on a stubborn old problem.

There's also the question of who's best qualified to diagnose a complex societal problem. For instance, if we were trying to solve teen pregnancy, whose perspectives would be more valuable in solving the problem: those who had achieved "success" in delaying pregnancy, or those who hadn't? Would we seek the opinions of women who started nuclear families at the age of thirty, to share their advice on how others can do the same?

Part of the reason we've failed to solve the gender gap is because the spotlight is on the trunk of the elephant, which we've mistaken for the whole animal. Do women who were born to be the boss suffer penalties for acting out of type? Absolutely. But would the majority of women say that being punished for their bossiness is the biggest obstacle to their career success? I doubt it. We've over-indexed our time and attention on problems that plague a smaller subset of women, while ignoring the ones that are more common and perhaps more troublesome. You can see them only if you zoom out to see the whole elephant. And that's why it's so important to hear various perspectives from women on all rungs of the corporate ladder.

Furthermore, many women don't see their challenges reflected in the modern campaign for gender equality. They don't identify with the women leading the conversation or connect with their message. But attempts to inject alternative points of view are almost always met with scorn and alienation. As a result, many women just keep their opinions to themselves.

The goal of this book is to uncover the truth about the gender gap. I'm not necessarily interested in who's right or who's wrong; I want to know what's true. To do that, I need to take my own advice and look at the elephant from other perspectives. So, before I share my own view on the issue, I wanted to better understand Sheryl Sandberg's. The popularity of *Lean In* has anointed Sandberg as the figurehead of modern-day feminism, and much of the country's understanding of the gender gap is born from the book's perspective.

I obviously can't get inside her brain and know exactly why she sees things the way she does, but I did the best I could to piece together her perspective. I read her speeches and books, watched her videos, and tried seeing success through the lens of her life experiences. Where is her perspective coming from, and how did it shape the message of *Lean In*—and by extension, modern-day feminism?

FROM BLIND MEN TO BLIND SPOTS

Let's home in on the cultural expectation that opened the chapter: bossiness. Throughout *Lean In*, Sandberg recounts several anecdotes about her desire to be in charge as a kid, and the negative reactions she received from those around her, including her siblings. She wrote that when people called her bossy, they didn't mean it as a compliment. Most women have experienced a similar sense of shame; for some it's liking sex too much, and for others it may be related to their appearance. Put in this light, almost every single woman can understand why

Sandberg would feel conflicted about her rise to power. The driving forces that have made her a huge success also violate the deeply held cultural norms that call for women, to quote singer-songwriter Daya, to "sit still, look pretty." It's unfair and unfortunate that women are punished time and time again for not being the docile creatures we're expected to be.

It also makes sense that Sandberg's solutions to empower women center on the idea that we women must flout society's expectations and embrace our inner boss. The message sprouts directly from her personal battles with a world that's not always fair and not always kind to women who want to be in charge. I genuinely sympathize with her position on many levels and feel similarly repulsed by arbitrary expectations that are put on women. My intention isn't to put her down. Rather, it's to demonstrate that the issues she's taking on are not only societal—they're deeply tied to her identity. When something as personal as identity is at stake, your beliefs become so strong that they turn into convictions.

People holding convictions feel certain about something and get angry if their conviction is questioned. They resist new input almost to the point of obsession. If they're powerful people, they'll use their power to prevent opposition and silence dissent. It isn't because they're bad people per se, but because the idea that they could be wrong feels too threatening.

According to author and motivational speaker Tony Robbins, "a conviction has usually been triggered by significant emotional events, during which the brain links up, 'Unless I believe this, I will suffer massive pain. *If* I were to change this belief, *then* I would be giving up my entire identity, everything my life has stood for, for years.' . . . [Convictions] can be dangerous because anytime we're not willing to even look at or consider the possibility that our beliefs are inaccurate, we trap ourselves in rigidity which could ultimately condemn us to long-term failure."[3]

That day in Detroit, in front of an audience of two hundred women, Sandberg told us to raise our hands if we were called bossy growing up. The reason she didn't seem interested in our answer is because it was never a question in the first place. It was an attempt to validate a conviction. To deal with the personal shame for her aggression, she likely assumes that every woman deep down is like her, all secretly yearning to be a CEO. But if 80 percent of that room had never been called bossy, what does it mean for her convictions on the gender gap? It means she might be wrong.

There's nothing inherently wrong with someone sharing his or her point of view. After all, that's what I'm doing with this book. And to be fair, it's hard for people to get out of their own perspective and see the bigger picture. But if people are truly and genuinely interested in helping others and solving a problem, then it doesn't matter whether their perspective is too narrow or their opinions are misguided. What matters more is that they encourage debate, tolerate dissent, and remain open to other points of view. A person's behavior in this regard hints at whether he or she is operating with a genuine desire to solve a problem, or with a desire to justify personal convictions and pursue his or her agenda.

Led by Sandberg, the public discourse on modern feminism has many hallmarks of a personal agenda, such as the attempt to control who is allowed to say what. The most notable example comes from LeanIn.org's nationwide campaign to ban the word *bossy*. Yes, an actual ban. On a *word*.

Banning the word *bossy* wasn't an offhand suggestion Sandberg made during a stump speech. It wasn't a joke taken out of context during a morning-show interview. It's a real campaign from LeanIn.org, in partnership with the Girl Scouts, to stop people from using the word *bossy* when referring to girls.

Can you think of anything bossier than telling people they can't use a word?

In *Lean In*, Sandberg explains that boys are rewarded for being vocal and opinionated, but women are called bossy. As a result of this double standard, she says that women mute their ambition, and men end up dominating conversations. Worse than the threat of authority figures silencing female voices, Sandberg contends, is that it causes women to "silence themselves."[4]

I'm all for being anti-authority, but what happens when the person drowning out other voices and silencing others is also a woman? What about banning the word *bossy*? Isn't that an example of an authority figure using her position to silence others?

Whether done by a man or a woman, controlling what people say is precisely the problem. It leads to the exclusion of some women in today's feminist discourse and borders on censorship, which is antithetical to the course of human progress.

Looking back on my experience at Facebook, the cultural tone under Sandberg's leadership wasn't exactly one of openness and objectivity. Compared to Google, where disagreement was tolerated if not encouraged, Facebook was drastically more controlling of *any* messaging, regardless of whether it was oppositional. It also wasn't just some abstract and harmless philosophical value. Draconian policies, coupled with vigilant enforcement, ensured a tight rein on messaging with our clients, and occasionally on stuff that wasn't even work related.

To wit, I once posted a story to my personal Medium blog about how creativity is crushed by linear business planning, and how egos stifle innovation. At the time, I had a total of three blog posts and an impressive global readership of four (50 percent being my parents). The blog contained only my name. It had no other personal information or social media connections, making it impossible to know who I was or where I worked. The word *Facebook* didn't appear in any of the three stories.

Despite the anonymity and nonexistent readership, one day I received an email from Facebook's corporate communications team asking me to delete the posts. I was dumbfounded. How did they even find them? And why would they care about a couple of anonymous posts, rotting in a desolate corner of the internet?

A friend of mine who runs HR at a large bank explained that big companies often employ tech firms to surface anything their employees post on the web. The purpose is for ~~big brother~~ the company to make sure that employees aren't posting anything that could ~~expose the truth~~ put them in legal trouble.

Figuring logic would prevail, I explained to the corporate communications rep that it was impossible to connect my stories to Facebook, that the posts were never shared on social media, and that I didn't actually say anything *about* Facebook. So, there was no reason to take them down. She responded that someone could do a "quick Google search" and connect my "views on big business" to Facebook.

I can only imagine the salacious headline that would have crushed the multibillion-dollar conglomerate:

**Unknown, Unimportant, Mid-Level Employee
at Facebook Posts Poorly Written Article
About the Negative Correlation Between
Creativity and Linear Planning Cycles**

Good job, Facebook! You really dodged the bullet and saved your ass on that one!

I understand that most big companies operate this way, and it makes sense to reduce exposure or liability. But when the intention is to remove *anything* they find disagreeable, even when it has nothing to do with them, it crosses the line from practicality into paranoid censorship.

Company culture is a reflection of its leaders. Sandberg's intent to control the voices of Facebook's employees is similar to her approach on women's issues.

Over the past twenty years, across both private and public sectors, tremendous amounts of resources, time, and attention have been invested in trying to promote more women into power. All the while, the numbers have barely budged. Female CEOs at *Fortune* 500 companies have gone from 0 percent in 1972 to 4.8 percent,[5] and the wage gap has narrowed from about 73 percent in 1998 to about 80 percent in 2018.[6] Despite the glacial—if nonexistent—progress, we continue hearing the same rhetoric from the same public figures. If we want to chart a new course, we need more voices and different perspectives, and perhaps most important, we need to sort the rhetoric from reality. We'll begin by reexamining the most well-known and widely accepted theory of modern-day feminism: the "leadership ambition gap."

FREE TO BE JUST LIKE ME

A girl should be two things: who and what she wants.

—COCO CHANEL

Several distinct agendas or factions of interest dwell under the umbrella of feminism. One of them centers on achieving gender equality through the legal system—equal rights and access to opportunity. In the nineteenth and early twentieth centuries, women fought for the right to vote and for equal access to education and the labor force. Whether women *wanted* to vote, *wanted* to go to college, or *wanted* to work was tangential. They now had the freedom to *decide for themselves*.

Another type of feminism contends that despite having equal rights and access, women remain oppressed by a patriarchal culture. In this school of thought, equality in America will be achieved only when men and women are the same in all respects. As Sandberg wrote in a Facebook post in March 2018: "An equal world will be one where women run half our countries and companies and men run half our homes."[1]

This brand of feminism isn't in the spirit of its "free to be you and me" predecessors. Rather, its essence is best captured in a quote by Rockefeller president Judith Rodin, used in *Lean In* to reflect Sandberg's own sentiment: "My generation fought so hard to give all of you choices. We believe in choices. But choosing to leave the workforce was not the choice we thought so many of you would make."[2]

In other words, we want you to have the freedom to choose what we think is best.

Today's feminist leaders define success for women on *their* terms: be just like them and choose the same paths to power. Because the majority of women aren't like them and don't define career success the same way, the effort is deemed a failure—of women, of society, of our true potential.

Unlike voting and reproductive rights, solutions for the gender gap can't be legislated. Women must *decide* they want to work harder for more money and more power, and then make the compromises necessary to go after it. But research shows that the majority of women *don't* want to be a CEO, and *don't* aspire to be a corporate executive to the same degree as men.[3] How do you close the gender gap and get more female CEOs if the majority of women say they don't want to be one? One way is to convince them that they can't possibly know what they want, without someone else's help.

Enter the leadership ambition gap.

While research consistently shows that men aspire to senior jobs more so than women, the reason why is the subject of much debate. The most popular and widely accepted answer is that leadership roles violate cultural norms for women. *Lean In* was the first to coin this phenomenon as the "leadership ambition gap."[4] Serving as the book's central thesis, the leadership ambition gap points to many ways that stereotypes and cultural conditioning are to blame for undermining women and their chances for success. For example, professional achievement is expected of men, but for women, it's considered optional at best, and at worst, they're punished for it. While Sandberg acknowledges other factors are at play, she points to culture as the main culprit: "Our desire for leadership is largely a culturally created and reinforced trait."[5]

The essence of the theory is that society rewards women for being warm, polite, compassionate, and nurturing and punishes them for male-dominant behavior, such as aggression, self-aggrandizement, and desire for dominance. The male traits are considered "leadership qualities," and because girls are penalized for exhibiting such qualities, Sandberg argues that they mute their ambition and grow less interested in leadership positions over time.

This cultural conditioning is said to start straight from the womb, where even as babies we treat boys and girls differently. As they grow up, we send our daughters the message that we don't expect much from them in the way of achievement. While we encourage our sons to achieve big things, we don't really care what our daughters do as long as they make us sandwiches and don't interrupt us while we're talking. Or something like that. The theory in short: when you train a nation of young girls to be subservient sheep, don't be surprised when they stay that way as adults.

Sandberg isn't alone in her belief that culture is to blame for the gender gap. The theory has practically defined the prevailing wisdom on the gender gap at companies like Google and Facebook, which developed many women's leadership efforts to ~~beat the crap out of our girl behaviors~~ empower their female employees.

Since many solutions to the gender gap are born from this strain of conventional wisdom, it's important to examine its validity. Is it true that women lack C-level aspirations because of culturally enforced stereotypes? Is the gender gap really the result of a society that punishes women for acting like leaders?

IT'S SOCIETY'S FAULT WE'RE INFERIOR!

At the heart of the leadership ambition gap is the damaging nature of stereotypes. Men are expected to be providers, to be bold, decisive, competitive, and ambitious, while women are expected to play the role of caregiver, to be nurturing, compassionate, and communal. In *Lean In*, Sandberg argues that this characterization of men and women as opposites leads us to place all aspects of professional achievement in the "male column."[6]

Women may suffer discrimination for violating a stereotype, but I posit that in the corporate world, we suffer a lot more by conforming to it. In the preceding descriptions of male and female stereotypes, which set of traits moves you up the corporate ladder? The nurturing, compassionate kind, or the decisive, driven kind? How many CEOs, male *or* female, are thought of as nurturing and compassionate? Stereotypical female traits don't get someone to the top of a large corporation—on that we probably all agree. But that means *fitting* the stereotype is far worse for a woman's career than *defying* it. Why is discrimination against nurturing, communal women okay, but discrimination against aggressive women is a national crisis?

Not only is the attempt to change millions of women a bad strategy for solving a problem, but the leadership ambition gap is laced with condescension, an attitude of "I know what's best for you," and "It's not your fault you're inferior—we can help."

Isn't that the exact *opposite* of empowerment?

Perhaps most disturbing of all is what the theory implies about men and women. Namely, that men represent the norm. The benchmark. The standard. That what they have, what they do, what they want is right, and women will never be truly equal to men unless we're exactly the same. In other words, the leadership ambition gap is built on a presumption of female inferiority.

———

Imagine that we asked women, "Do you aspire to be a corporate executive or CEO?" If the majority of women answered yes, then helping them climb the corporate ladder would make sense and be a worthy endeavor. However, as previously stated, the majority of women have said no, they don't want to be corporate executives. The leadership ambition gap works by disregarding the answers as irrelevant, suggesting that the only reason women say no is because they're culturally conditioned to say that. Taking our thoughts, feelings, and desires into consideration is pointless, I suppose.

This dismissal of what women want is another reason the public discourse on the gender gap lacks honesty. In private, between good friends, we freely admit feeling apathetic or conflicted about our careers. At work, or in public, we wouldn't dare. Admitting ambivalence or being tentative about your ambition is seen as foolish surrender to the culture trying to keep us down. Instead, we repeat the narrative handed to us by the women in charge of the conversation.

The dismissal of women's desires also leaves a question mark in its place, a blank that can be filled by anyone with an agenda. This is precisely why so many women's leadership events feel more like feminist theater than anything else. If all you're expected to do is repeat rhetoric, anyone with an agenda or interest in self-promotion can take the stage and act as if he or she is truly interested in your well-being.

The second aspect of the leadership ambition gap is captured in the corresponding chapter's subtitle: "What Would You Do If You Weren't Afraid?"[7] Sandberg believes that "fear is at the root of so many of the barriers that women face" suggesting that without it, we could pursue success unencumbered.[8]

Instead of me telling you my opinion on this (I'm a girl, so you'll have to excuse me for my reticence), let's ask ourselves the questions: What *would* I do if I weren't afraid? What would my career be like if I could release the fears holding me back?

Did you think to yourself, *Hmm. If I weren't afraid, I'd become the CEO of a multinational conglomerate!* or, *I'd finally go after that seat on the executive board of a Wall Street hedge fund I've always dreamed about*? If so, then God bless you and Godspeed, sister. I'm just not sure you're reading the right book.

How many of us, if we weren't afraid, would lean into our jobs until we reached our dream of becoming a corporate executive? It's almost laughable. Being a corporate CEO isn't bad. But the assumption that deep down, we really aspire toward that kind of role, shows how out of touch Sandberg is with the hearts and minds of women.

Furthermore, if Sandberg *is* right, what would be the cure for this CEO-anxiety infecting the country's females? The antidote, she suggests, is for women to face their fears and take risks. Sandberg notes that at Facebook, they work very hard to create an environment that encourages this kind of bold, risk-taking behavior in its female employees.[9]

That's great advice and applies to more than just women. But getting people to face their fears isn't simple or easy. How they accomplish such a feat holds great promise for the rest of corporate America. If we can learn what the leader of modern feminism is doing to super-size female ambition in her own backyard, surely we can model her approach and make a meaningful impact across other large companies.

So, how *does* Sandberg encourage such a significant behavioral change in the thousands of female Facebookers?

"We have posters all around the office that reinforce this attitude."[10]

Posters. The leader of modern-day feminism, running one of the largest and most famous public companies in the world, helps solve the leadership ambition gap with *posters*.

―――――――

If it's not cultural conditioning, stereotype threat, societal expectations, or fear, then why *don't* women want to be CEOs as much as men do? Have we ever considered that the answer might be that women simply don't want to be CEOs? Less than 25 percent of America's teachers are men.[11] Do we treat it as a societal issue that must be fixed? Why, then, do we judge only women's ambition as good or bad? Why do we create national campaigns urging women to advance up the corporate ladder without taking into consideration whether it's something they want to do?

In a McKinsey study titled *Women in the Workplace*, the researchers surveyed thousands of men and women about their attitudes toward being a top executive. The top reasons cited for not wanting to be a senior executive were

- I wouldn't be able to balance family and work commitments (42 percent women, 42 percent men);
- Too much politics (39 percent women, 40 percent men); and
- I am not interested in that type of work (35 percent women, 37 percent men).[12]

Do these reasons seem unreasonable? Culturally conditioned? It's interesting that, for the most part, men don't want to be a corporate executive for the same reasons women don't. Is culture at play for them too? The same study also reports that 36 percent of men desire a C-level position, versus 18 percent of women. That means the majority of the population, men *and* women, don't want to be a CEO. Doesn't it make more sense to look at what might be wrong with the job instead of what's wrong with all the *people* who don't want it?

Even if the leadership ambition gap were true, and women *are* delicate creatures vulnerable to self-deception, I'm still not sure I understand the implications. To figure out what women really want, we should stop listening to society and start listening to Sheryl Sandberg? It's so confusing to be a woman!

To reiterate, am I saying that culture and stereotypes don't affect our choices? No. I'm saying that we have clung so tightly to the notion that our lack of ambition is culturally created, that we dismiss and ignore other valid, and perhaps larger, reasons for the gender gap. Instead of dismissing women's stated desires, we should take them seriously and see if they point to clues about the overall problem. For example, McKinsey reports that one of the reasons women don't want to be a CEO is "not enough benefits for the personal costs."[13] This reasonable statement is certainly worthy of further exploration, no? What kinds of benefits *would* make it worth the cost? Is there something broken about rewards and incentives? This kind of inquiry would be far more helpful in solving the problem. Instead, women's concerns are summarily dismissed as a product of cultural oppression.

THE DOMESTIC AMBITION GAP

For two years at Google, I sat across from a guy named Ed. Our area resembled a trading desk more than it did a corporate office—no closed-door offices or cubicle walls—so I had an unfettered view of Ed. And he fascinated me. For those two years I studied Ed the way I imagine Jane Goodall studied chimpanzees in the wild. After arriving every morning at 6:45 a.m., he'd set down his stuff, open his laptop, and get right to work. Except for meetings and the occasional food break, he stared at his computer, without looking up, then abruptly packed up his things and walked out the door at 7:30 p.m.

Perhaps the reason I found Ed so intriguing was because, like me, he had three kids, about the same age as mine. Unlike me, Ed didn't seem to think about his kids during work hours. I'm not saying that judgmentally, but as a matter-of-fact observation. Ed's wife, Leslie (with whom I ended up becoming good friends, and not just for research purposes), was a stay-at-home mom. She spent her days running the household and managing the kids' schoolwork and schedules, and rarely, if ever, bothered Ed with any kid-related stuff during the work-week. The division of labor in their home allowed Ed to put his whole self into his job, every day, for more than twelve hours a day. While I never envied Ed's obsessive work habits, I did envy his arrangement with Leslie. Ed was able to make it to every single meeting in person. He never knew what it was like to miss a half day of work for parent-teacher conferences. Unlike me, a school nurse had never called him in the middle of a presentation. He had the time and the mental space to be present at the office and devoted to business during business hours.

After observing this about Ed, I started to notice the trend among other men at work, particularly the senior executives. It wasn't that they all had stay-at-home wives—many of them didn't; their wives also worked. But the vast majority of them didn't stretch their mental energy across kids, home life, and work life in the same way that I and many of my female colleagues did. Perhaps the fact that we were pulling more weight, playing double-duty roles, wouldn't have had such an impact on our careers if we also weren't trying to cover it up, pretending that in addition to our jobs, we weren't also responsible for the majority of domestic chores and child-rearing. The expectation was to act as if we had it all under control, and that our time was an endless, inexhaustible resource. Yet if you listened to the private conversations between moms in the hallways, or in bars after work, we'd all confess that what we truly needed, to be more successful at work, was a wife.

It's well understood and widely accepted that a major reason why women don't get higher up the ladder at work is because they're responsible for the majority of chores at home. Even women who work full-time are typically the primary caregivers as well, and still do a disproportionate amount of domestic work.[14] These figures haven't changed much in recent years, despite women entering the workforce en masse. Obviously, *someone* would have to pick up the extra responsibilities if women are spending more time leaning into their careers, but the effort to get men to lean in more at home has been conspicuously absent from the public conversation. While the leadership ambition gap tries to explain why women don't want to be CEOs, what is the corollary for men who don't want to assume more responsibility at home or act as the primary caregiver to the children? Is the reason they prefer to spend more time at work purely due to the stereotype of man as breadwinner? Are they victims of cultural conditioning? Or do they simply prefer not to be more involved in domestic pursuits?

Whatever the answers are, it demonstrates another dimension to how the causes and solutions to the gender gap fall on women's shoulders. Even though we know men must pick up the slack at home and change their behavior to achieve the stated goal of "half our businesses, half our homes," we never ask them to do anything different in any significant way. Instead, we remain relentlessly focused on the female part of the equation.

Perhaps an even more salient point is that women's choices are subject to dismissal and condescension in a way men's are not. We blame stereotypes for the lack of women running big corporations, but we never talk about stereotypes for the lack of men running our homes. Or if this stereotype gets mentioned here and there, no serious efforts are made to break men free of their supposed cultural conditioning. We aren't as quick to dismiss men's behavior. I've never seen McKinsey do a study on all the reasons men don't want to participate at home, then explain the results as products of culture.

Throughout history, people have told women how to behave. In the first half of the twentieth century, women's books and magazines were virtually instruction manuals telling women how to conduct themselves as wives and mothers. For example, in his 1943 book *Sex Today in Wedded Life*, author Edward Podolsky provides a list of commandments women must follow in order to be considered a "good wife," which includes the following:

- "Don't bother your husband with petty troubles and complaints when he comes home from work.
- Be a good listener. Let him tell you his troubles; yours will seem trivial in comparison.
- Remember your most important job is to build up and maintain his ego (which gets bruised plenty in business). Morale is a woman's business.
- Let him relax before dinner. Discuss family problems after the inner man has been satisfied."[15]

Almost eighty years later, these instructions seem ridiculous, a relic from a time long gone.

But isn't telling women to speak more assertively and to drop the emotional language a different version of the same instruction? The advice might be aimed at different roles (work vs. family), but we're still offering women prescriptions on how to behave in a way we rarely do with men.

As we'll see in later chapters, some of the most mainstream "feminist" books on the shelves *today* include directives such as *"Don't feed people at the office"* and *"Don't be too nice."*[16] History is littered with examples of women being told who to be, while men are considered fine the way they are. The leadership ambition gap is a shiny wrapper on the same tradition. It excuses the changes required of men, while providing a detailed guide for how women should behave and a theory on why they're not behaving that way in the first place. If the leadership ambition gap were true, then *Lean In* should have captured men's reticence toward domestic responsibility in a chapter titled "The Domestic Ambition Gap."

LEADERSHIP THEATER

For a number of years at Google, I was part of what's called a "sales enablement" team. We weren't direct sellers, but we were given the same quota as the sales teams we supported. That meant we had to help them sell: anything we could do to make their job easier or help them bring in more business was considered a success.

A couple of us had tested a new partnership idea that resulted in significant efficiencies in the order process. The sales teams were ecstatic; their clients were happier, and it freed up hours of time to devote to selling-related activities, instead of order processing. Since it was only a test, but a highly promising one, we created a presentation of the results to share with our vice president, Jonathan. We imagined how thrilled he'd be at the results and daydreamed about our next promotion.

In a small conference room, Jonathan looked over the slides and smiled as we presented the details of what we'd done. A hint of amusement was on his face, as if we were his kids coming home from elementary school to share our "All about Me" project from arts and crafts. And like a father, he gave us a "Nice job" and a perfunctory pat on the head. If he could have, I imagine he would've ended the meeting with, "Okay, kids. Run along now."

Jonathan never mentioned the project again. Ever. He didn't approve our request to bring the same solution to other teams that could have equally benefited. What could've been easily replicated for ten times the results died quietly on the vine. What could've made a revenue impact in the millions never saw the light of day. The salespeople continued with a laborious deal process, and life went on. I was dumbfounded.

It wasn't until much later, after I'd gotten to know Jonathan much better and was more fluent in office politics, that I finally understood his reaction. The project, although it achieved massive results, created the image that our team was merely in service of sales. That we were *helpers*. Indentured servants for the teams that did the *real* work. Jonathan's peers were vice presidents of sales. The last thing his ego could tolerate was them viewing him as their bitch.

The fix for our sales problem was simple. But fixing it required leadership to be interested in solving the problem. Jonathan wasn't a bad guy. He wasn't trying to make things hard for the salespeople. However, his self-worth and image were at stake, and the project threatened his ego.

At the time, I thought Jonathan's behavior was self-defeating—bad for his career and bad for the company. The company saw it otherwise. He was promoted faster than most VPs his level and eventually moved to a large role managing a profit and loss of almost half a billion dollars. Turns out Jonathan knew exactly what he was doing.

I'm not taking the moral high ground here. I don't feel any sort of ethical superiority to the machinations of corporate America. I didn't care *what* game we were playing. I just wanted everyone to be honest about it and stop pretending that what we were doing had some inherent logical sense. We were mostly moving papers from one side of the desk to the other and building castles made of sand. Yet every day, we put on our costumes, entered stage left, and pretended to be building the Sistine Chapel.

When we look at what corporate ambition entails and what it requires of people, it makes you wonder whether the lack of female executives is a positive reflection on women. The winners of the corporate game are simply the ones who play it best. It doesn't mean they're leaders.

Wanting to be a corporate executive isn't "leadership ambition." It's "executive ambition." Like a man who wants to be a college professor has "academic ambition." Ambition is a big goal, an aspiration, an objective, a purpose, a plan. Ambition can be applied to anything. Motherhood, writing, cleanliness, wealth, fitness. If people don't want to be a corporate CEO, it doesn't mean they don't have ambition. It means they don't have ambition to be a CEO.

And what about leadership, which is a universally positive aspiration? How could anyone in their right mind not support more women becoming leaders? Opposing the idea appears sexist by default. The problem, however, is that a leader isn't the same thing as a corporate executive. Most people don't follow their CEO (or even their manager) because they believe in that leader's vision and want to join his or her cause. They do it because they have to; the power structure requires it. It's more than a little unwise to disobey people who can destroy your career on a whim.

Let's take one of the most highly respected, widely admired, and celebrated leaders of the twentieth century, Martin Luther King Jr. A master of influence who inspired millions of people to follow his lead, MLK ignited a revolution in social justice. Nobody would argue that aspiring toward that kind of leadership and influence requires enormous ambition, the kind worthy of our encouragement not only for women but for any human being.

When we hear the term *leadership*, we almost always conjure up images of people such as MLK and Abraham Lincoln, who are worthy of our aspiration. But if you have ambition to become a leader in the spirit of MLK and exert influence on a global scale, corporate executives are last on the list of people you should study. A corporate CEO's power is formal authority over others. The first implies choice, and the second control. The people who followed MLK didn't work for him. He didn't hold any formal power over them. He led with influence. He made people feel heard and understood. He painted a vision of a better future and motivated his followers to act. People *chose* to follow MLK because he commanded respect, engendered trust, and deserved their admiration. Dr. King embodies the cocktail of traits from which true leaders are born.

CEOs, on the other hand, don't arrive at their position by the will of the people. They don't acquire more and more power on their way to the top because they possess the same leadership qualities as an MLK. Their subordinates don't listen to and obey their commands out of choice; they don't act out of a personal belief in their manager's mission. They follow a corporate leader because they have to. Their livelihood, and in many cases their self-worth, depends on it.

MLK and a corporate CEO represent two distinct and diametrically opposed forms of leadership. When we say that men want to be CEOs more than women do, that statement doesn't represent women's lack of ambition toward being leaders. It reflects a lack of desire to be a CEO, or to be an executive with lots of authority and control over other people.

Treating the difference as a societal problem implies that C-level status is an inherently worthwhile endeavor. But it's only worthy for those who aspire to that status. For the rest of us, meh. Personally, I've never looked at the top levels of the organizations I worked for and seen that many people I aspired to be. I've seen people I was afraid of. Or who were assholes. Or who were bad at their jobs but amazing at managing up. Yes, there were good eggs, too, and some I admired very much. But most of the impressive people, the ones who embodied the leadership ideal, never seemed to make it to the top.

THREE

THE CONFIDENCE GAP

If you want anything said, ask a man. If you want anything done, ask a woman.

—MARGARET THATCHER

Another big thread of conventional wisdom on the gender gap is that compared to men, women lack confidence, and therefore, they're not as successful. Consistent with the trend of giving each flavor of female inferiority its own name, this one has been coined "the confidence gap." The theory tells us that confidence is equally important to competence when it comes to success. Because women don't have as much confidence as men, they're less apt to ask for raises, negotiate salaries, and seize opportunities, and are less likely to be seen as "leadership material" in the workplace.

But what is confidence? Is it true that men have more? And if this is true, does this difference contribute to the country's gender and wage gap?

CONFIDENCE AND SUCCESS

A study by Joyce Ehrlinger and David Dunning at Cornell University is often cited as damning evidence that not only do women lack confidence compared to men, but the difference plays a central role in women's failure to break the glass ceiling.[1] The study examines two main questions: Do men think more highly of themselves? And if so, do they go after more opportunities as a result? The study uses the "seizing of opportunities" as a proxy for success. In other words, if women fail to pursue opportunities because they don't believe they're well equipped, it can explain a lot about why they don't get ahead as often in business.

To answer these questions, Ehrlinger and Dunning designed the following experiment in two parts. First, a group of college students were asked to rate their skill from 1 to 10 in the area of "scientific reasoning," then take a short quiz on the subject. Despite the fact that on average, women rated their skills in scientific reasoning lower than men (6.5 versus 7.6, respectively[2]), both genders performed similarly well on the quiz. Based on these results, Ehrlinger and Dunning drew their first conclusion: women suffer from lower levels of confidence than men.

Let's put aside for a moment the fact that confidence in *general* is not at all the same as confidence in *scientific reasoning*. That's an almost unforgivable error of logic for a scientific study, but the magnitude of negligence only gets worse, and we have only so much time.

The second part of the experiment was designed to test whether or not women's purported lack of confidence impacted their willingness to pursue related opportunities. After the self-assessment and the quiz, participants were invited to enter a *Jeopardy!*-style contest on the same topic of scientific reasoning. Only 49 percent of the women signed up to compete, versus 71 percent of the men. This difference, coupled with the results from the first part of the experiment, led Ehrlinger and Dunning to conclude, "Because [women] are less confident in general in their abilities, that led them not to want to pursue future opportunities."[3]

Uh . . . what?

Let's recap what just happened here. Students were asked if they want to participate in a contest about science. Fewer women said yes. So, the researchers concluded that it was because they lacked confidence.

I'm not an organizational psychologist, but if I were in charge of such a study, I'm pretty sure I'd try to rule out other possible reasons why the women didn't want to participate in a science competition. For example, I might ask:

- Do you give a shit about science?
- Do you give enough shits about it that you'd choose to spend your free time in a contest on it?

Or how about simply asking:

- Why don't you want to participate in the contest?

Lest we forget, these were college students. Had I been given this "opportunity" in college, I absolutely would've turned it down. Not because I don't think I'm good at science, but because I had higher priorities in my life. Like partying.

To demonstrate just how ridiculous this study's results are, consider a hypothetical. Let's say the study was replicated, and everything was the same, except the topic was nursing instead of scientific reasoning.

Suppose men rated their ability to nurse and care for patients at a 6.5 (versus 7.6 for women), and they also declined the competition at a higher rate than women. Can you imagine the headline for the study? "Men Underrepresented in Nursing Profession Due to Lack of Confidence."

When women are disinterested in something like science, it's a societal disease. When men are disinterested in anything, nobody freaking cares.

People might say that STEM (science, technology, engineering, and math) careers are the future of the economy, and it's critical for women to participate. But that's a value judgment. It reflects the weight our culture puts on money; it's not a reflection of what role is more valuable to society. Is an engineer inherently more worthy than a nurse? Furthermore, this idea demonstrates our tendency to blame women for "failing" to adopt the same interests, dreams, and careers as men. We declare it a defect that must be fixed. The reverse—fewer men interested or participating in female-dominated fields—is never seen as a deficiency. We accept it as is.

The term "confidence gap" first gained traction in the mainstream when it appeared as the title in an *Atlantic* article by Katty Kay and Claire Shipman, based on their book *The Confidence Code: The Science and Art of Self-Assurance—What Women Should Know*. While Kay and Shipman admit that things like motherhood, culture, and institutional barriers play large roles in women's failure to break the glass ceiling, they claim we're missing a much bigger reason: lack of confidence. They explain that compared to men, women underestimate themselves, feel like frauds, predict they'll fare worse on tests, and believe they're less deserving of opportunities and credit. Kay and Shipman also blame women's lack of confidence for the country's wage and earnings gap, claiming that men ask for raises and negotiate salary more frequently than their female colleagues.

On its surface, their argument doesn't seem far-fetched. The terms *alpha male* and *male ego* are common acknowledgments of the boldness with which men assert themselves. And it's also not hard to see why such displays are helpful in climbing the corporate ladder. Aggression is almost a prerequisite for winning.

Kay and Shipman open *The Confidence Code* with a plea to their female readers: "Start acting . . . and stop mumbling and apologizing and prevaricating."[4] They say that this behavior—this fumbling, moronic laziness—which they call "lack of confidence," is the reason we don't earn as much money as men or make it to the top of the nation's largest power structures. If you're trying to increase our confidence, describing us as shady, meek, and inactive isn't how I'd begin. But let's give this idea the benefit of the doubt and move on for now.

Since the entire premise of *The Confidence Code* is that women are less successful than men because we're less confident, it's critical to understand how Kay and Shipman define confidence. The second sentence of the introduction provides a clue, describing confidence as "hard to define but easy to recognize."[5] I had hoped to get more clarity by the end of chapter 1, but instead of a concrete definition, the authors offer a series of anecdotes to describe what it looks like when women lack confidence:

You'd love to give a thoughtful toast at your best friend's birthday party, but even the prospect of speaking in front of thirty people makes you start to sweat—so you mutter a few words, keep it very short, and nurse a dissatisfied feeling that you haven't done her justice. You always wished you'd run for class president in college, but asking other people to vote for you, well, it just seemed so arrogant. Your brother-in-law is so annoying with his sexist views, but you're worried that if you stand up to him in front of everyone you'll come across as strident, and, anyway, he always seems so on top of his facts.[6]

I'm not a psychiatrist, but aren't these like . . . *human* things? Surveys show that the fear of public speaking is the number one fear among everyone in the world. It ranks higher than the fear of death![7] Also, is there some national crisis I didn't know about where women are afraid to . . . complain . . . about their families?

To crystalize confidence's elusive nature, Kay and Shipman provide a series of contrasting descriptions of how it shows up, or fails to show up, across gender. I distilled the various anecdotes into their essence, which look something like this:

Confidence in men

- A quality that sets some people apart, which is hard to define but easy to recognize
- Self-belief

Lack of confidence in women

- Mumbling, apologizing, and prevaricating
- Too much humility
- Self-doubt
- Inexplicable feeling that they don't fully own their right to rule the top
- Fear that if they speak out, they will sound either stupid or self-aggrandizing
- The sense that their success is unexpected and undeserved
- Anxiety about leaving their comfort zone to try something exciting and hard and possibly risky
- Lack of self-belief

By page 35, I was ashamed to be a woman. Mercifully, the authors arrive at a concrete definition of confidence fifteen pages later. Phew.

I was starting to lose hope that we'd capture this mysterious female deficiency in any sort of concrete way. After stating all the ways women are ~~annoying, inept losers~~ less confident, Kay and Shipman define confidence as "the stuff that turns thought into action."[8]

Wait—am I reading *The Secret*?

The notion that women can't turn thoughts into action as well as men is not only wrong; it's insulting. Many of the women I know are virtual heroes—managing their households, doing the majority of child-rearing, and somehow still making it to the office every day and working just as hard as everyone else. When my three kids were babies, I went through a traumatic divorce and was forced to take care of them, the house, a move, a court case, and a full-time, demanding job at Google on my own. Did I get a good score that quarter at work? Hell no. But was anything about me *inactive*?

Without a practical, working definition of confidence, I instead turned my attention to the descriptions and anecdotes of confident behavior in *The Confidence Code*. The book includes dozens of stories in which men are described as commanding the room, projecting an air of certitude, and remaining unwavering in their belief. In the face of such "confidence," women often shut down, become tentative, or share their opinions only when they're 100 percent sure they're right.

One example is the story of David Rodriguez, a VP of human resources at Marriott, and the authors' go-to management guru. After telling us how awesome he is, they turn to Rodriguez for his perspective on this whole messy female confidence issue. Turns out he agrees that confidence is what makes or breaks someone's rise to the top of the corporate ladder. Rodriguez says that he sees his female colleagues often do something he calls "a hesitation." For example, he has seen more than one woman become tentative during a key point of their presentation. Afterward, when he asks them why they hesitated, they say something along the lines of "I couldn't get a feel for the audience—how they were responding. I couldn't decide whether to go right or left."[9]

When did being uncertain about stuff you're uncertain about become something terrible? If the women on Rodriguez's team want to get promoted, must they lie about what they know and what they believe? Do they have to feign certainty, even when important business matters are at stake? There's another way to look at the hesitation Rodriguez describes. When I read the comment "I couldn't get a feel for the audience," my first thought wasn't that the women lacked confidence, but that they were demonstrating empathy. Most women are naturally skilled in taking the temperature of a room, getting a sense for how others are feeling, and taking these things into account. In the most recent stable of business literature, these so-called soft skills are touted as the necessary leadership skills for today's information economy. With female-dominant strengths such as empathy and consensus-building being the future of business, the headlines forecast that women will dominate the future generations of corporate leaders. But that won't happen until we stop mistaking empathy for weakness.

I'm not suggesting that hesitating mid-presentation is something to strive for per se, nor am I saying it's always a signal of empathy. I'm pointing out that hesitation can be caused by many things, some good, some bad. It's not a clear-cut indication that one lacks confidence. Once a narrative like "women are less confident than men" becomes accepted as truth, it's easy for people to interpret any behavior as evidence.

In another story, a man who was a senior partner at a law firm described a junior female associate who rarely spoke up during meetings.[10] He chalked it up to a lack of confidence. Because she didn't talk as much as the others in the room, he assumed she believed she couldn't handle the account. This bothered him, but even more so because he didn't feel he could talk to her about the issue without offending her.

Instead of speaking with her directly about it, he made "confidence" a required part of the formal review process, since he thinks it's such an important aspect of doing business.

I find it ironic that when his female colleague didn't speak up in meetings, he assumed she lacked confidence, yet when he didn't speak up about his concern, it was because he was being sensitive to her feelings. Instead of having the confidence to discuss the matter with her directly, this man changed the entire performance-review process to prevent anyone from being quiet in meetings, ever again.

On the flip side of girly behavior, there's the story of Maj. Gen. Jessica Wright. General Wright is the picture-perfect vision of female confidence, the precise kind of female role model the authors want to inspire women to be. Kay and Shipman describe her as "resolutely feminine" (her favorite leadership tip is to enjoy getting your hair and nails done), but without all that yucky hesitating stuff. Wright doesn't tolerate that sort of thing. She says she doesn't have time for indecisive or uncertain people, and she appears to have a near disdain for those who admit they don't have all the answers. General Wright is also one of the people the authors turned to for help in defining confidence, and her personality traits helped them arrive at a more solid understanding of the term. Leaving their meeting, Kay and Shipman describe her in their notebooks with words such as *action, bold, honest,* and *feminine.*[11]

WHAT IS CONFIDENCE?

It's incredibly hard to examine a theory about confidence without a clear definition of the term. It's a common word that means different things to different people. Kay and Shipman claim confidence is the ability to turn thought into action. But that describes a fundamental process of how human beings navigate the world. If I think, *I need to wash the dishes*, and then proceed to the kitchen to begin washing said dishes, according to *The Confidence Code*, I'm demonstrating confidence. This might seem like quibbling over semantics, but there can't be a thoughtful examination of a theory without first agreeing on what it means.

Over the years I've read dozens of books on psychology, identity, and the nature of the human ego. Throughout the scientific literature, there's a loose consensus on confidence, so I looked to the research for a more workable definition. Psychotherapist Nathaniel Branden, PhD, was a pioneer in the area of self-esteem and confidence, and his groundbreaking work serves as the foundation for modern psychology's understanding of the subject. In his seminal book *The Six Pillars of Self-Esteem*, Branden defines self-esteem as feeling that one is worthy of happiness and competent to face life, with all its requirements. More specifically, he says, self-esteem is

1. "confidence in our ability to think, confidence in our ability to cope with the basic challenges of life; and
2. confidence in our right to be successful and happy, the feeling of being worthy, deserving, entitled to assert our needs and wants, achieve our values, and enjoy the fruits of our efforts."[12]

In this regard, confidence means trusting oneself. It is trusting in one's ability to think, to learn, to make appropriate choices and decisions, and to respond effectively to change. People with a healthy confidence level *act* in the face of uncertainty because they trust the efficacy of their minds. It doesn't mean they *never feel uncertain*, and it doesn't mean they *never appear uncertain*. It's the opposite: Confident people feel *comfortable* hesitating when they're hesitant. They don't feel threatened by not having all the answers.

One of the most important things to understand is that self-trust is predicated on honesty. True confidence requires an *honest* relationship with yourself—a willingness to acknowledge your talents and strengths, and the courage to see and accept the things you lack. It doesn't mean you believe you're the best or have some delusional idea that you can do *anything*. It means you have a realistic understanding of who you are, and you trust in your strength, ability, and fortitude to survive challenges in pursuit of the things you want.

If there's an opposite of confidence, it's ego. Ego is born of self-*deception* and feeds on illusion. Confidence is loyalty to the truth, while ego is loyalty to being right. It's artifice and facade, and it can be measured by how willing we are to lie to ourselves and others about what we know to be true. Ego, in the form of arrogance and bravado, projects the illusion of confidence. But it's a strategy to compensate for the fact that you don't have any.

Like Kay and Shipman, Branden emphasizes the importance of action as it relates to confidence. However, according to Branden, the difference between high and low confidence is what *motivates* the action. When action emerges from self-honesty and acceptance of reality, it's confidence. When it's born of one's refusal of reality, an unwillingness to accept some truth, it's low confidence. Any behavior in isolation is a meaningless indication of one's confidence. What *really* matters is whether it's born from truth or delusion.[13]

When people don't trust the efficacy of their minds, their ability to think, they often overcompensate by deluding themselves into believing they're good at everything. The workplace is littered with people who need to be right, all the time. Everyone can think of at least one person they've worked with who dominates every meeting with an air of arrogant certainty. Behind the veneer of self-righteousness is someone who's trying to control all elements in his environment and all the people on his team, in a desperate effort to mitigate uncertainty. Not having the right answer to your question or not saying the right thing feels threatening to a person like that. He sees it as confirmation that he's failing in some way. The best strategy is to keep talking, dominate the conversation, so there's no room for you to see that he might not really know what he's talking about. He's not confident. He's *afraid*. The arrogance is a veneer, a guard he won't let down for fear that people might see through him and know he doesn't have it all together.

When a person has little trust in his or her ability to deal with risk or the day-to-day challenges of living, everything can feel like a threat. Life becomes a treacherous journey, with uncertainty and failure as the enemies. Those with little confidence wear certainty and arrogance like armor, shielding themselves from the abyss of unknowns.

The opposite of false bravado is false modesty. People who see themselves as less than they truly are often undermine themselves, refusing to take action in situations where they're perfectly capable of doing so. We tend to refer to people like this as having an "inferiority complex," and they come off as lacking assertiveness, displaying behaviors such as subservience and timidity.

False bravado and false modesty manifest in opposite behaviors, but they spring from the same source: low confidence. Kay and Shipman argue that women need to drop their hesitation and timidity in favor of unwarranted certitude and bravado, seemingly unaware that these traits are caused by the same wellspring of insecurities.

In *The Six Pillars of Self-Esteem*, Branden describes confident behaviors as correlating with rationality, realism, creativity, independence, willingness to admit and correct mistakes, cooperativeness, and flexibility. In contrast, he describes lack of confidence as correlating with irrationality, blindness to reality, rigidity, overcontrolling behavior, inappropriate conformity, and fear or hostility toward others.[14] If confidence underpins the first set of behaviors, fear drives the second set.

As such, confidence requires you to trust your mind, think for yourself, ask why, reject dogma, and refuse adherence to blind authority. In that sense, confidence would appear to be a *liability* in the corporate world! It can't thrive in a system entirely defined by a chain of command that requires the overwhelming majority of people to obey authority, lest they compromise their livelihood, financial security, and personal identity. The corporate world's power structures reward bravado and crush confidence. And *that* is the real gap we should be trying to address.

CONFIDENCE MATTERS MOST

One assumption underlying the confidence gap theory is that when it comes to being successful, confidence matters more than talent, intellect, effort, and competence. Because women are purported to have less confidence, this lack takes a devastating toll on their ability to succeed. Furthermore, it's why so many female leadership programs focus on building confidence. It's believed that closing the confidence gap will, in turn, close the larger gender gap in corporate America.

If we follow the logic of this assumption, that more confidence equals more success, it means that the most successful people—ones with the most money and power in society—have the most confidence. But is that true? I think many of us have met at least one rich, powerful person who also happened to reek of insecurity. There are models who lack confidence in their beauty, and there are Nobel Prize winners who lack confidence in their intellect. Acquiring things, whether power, money, fame, or beauty, isn't a sign of confidence. This isn't to say that confidence isn't a catalyst for success, but it's not such a neat, linear relationship, as the confidence gap theory implies.

Of course, we can't ignore the fact that sometimes a crazy, irrational belief about what one is capable of accomplishing helps someone achieve said accomplishment. For example, to start Microsoft, Bill Gates sold his BASIC software to a company in Albuquerque before he, or anyone else in the world, had created it. Putting himself on the line with no evidence he was capable of such a feat was exactly the kind of chutzpah needed to start his computer empire. Isn't this evidence that outsized confidence or bravado is necessary for success? The confidence Gates had in starting Microsoft was born from a desire to achieve great things and a belief that he could handle any obstacles along the way. It wasn't bred from self-delusion, but from self-belief. It's certitude along the lines of "I will achieve my dreams because I have what it takes to work hard and handle failure"—in contrast to the false and unwarranted certitude of "I need to convince people that I'm the best and that I'm always right, because if they believe it, I won't have to be tested." Although the latter may enable hollow "achievements," these mostly serve as a way to fill a bottomless pit of insecurity. One could hardly call this success.

Am I saying that women shouldn't try practicing self-assertion? Obviously not. I've personally benefited from the endeavor. My point is that the gender gap isn't the result of some mysterious female deficit, like lack of confidence, that can be easily solved by acting more like men.

DO MEN HAVE MORE CONFIDENCE?

Another area that warrants further exploration is the idea that men have more confidence than women. In particular, I was curious about how proponents of the theory arrived at their conclusion. We touched on this in the beginning of the chapter with the study by Ehrlinger and Dunning, but surely other studies, research, or bodies of work must exist. The theory couldn't have been built on the results of one study.

Given that the entire premise of *The Confidence Code* is built on the assumption that men do, in fact, have more confidence than women, I started by digging deeper to understand how Kay and Shipman arrived at the conclusion. Did they send out surveys, with a large enough sample size, and find statistically significant results? Perform lab research? Analyze existing studies to look for patterns?

Turns out, they talked to a bunch of people. To clarify, I don't mean they took detailed scientific observations and codified the results into a replicable study. They talked to a bunch of people about the topic of confidence, and the women with whom they spoke admitted a struggle with confidence much more so than the men.

I'm not dismissing their results because of their unscientific approach. I'm dismissing it because it's easy to see how they could validate a claim they already believed to be true. Aren't women usually more open with their thoughts and feelings, more willing to discuss their insecurities with other women? Just imagine some male executive sitting down across the table from two women writing a book about confidence, and being asked if he ever feels insecure at work. "Oh yes. I have many deep-seated fears about not being good enough." Said no man, ever.

Throughout the book, Kay and Shipman refer to the frequency with which insecurity came up in conversations with women compared to men. From there, they draw an all-too-linear conclusion: women have less confidence. But maybe it came up more often with women because women are more self-aware. And maybe men brought it up less because they lack self-awareness and aren't in tune with themselves well enough to see the connection between their aggression and their insecurities.

Basing a theory of this nature on a bunch of people self-reporting their experiences, without a cross section of meaningful research—and without a clear definition of confidence—isn't exactly the bedrock of evidence necessary to support such an argument.

In pursuit of other research, I was reminded again of the McKinsey study mentioned in chapter 2. Of the most often cited reasons for why both men and women don't want to be top executives, "I'm not confident that I would be successful" appears last on the list. The percent of women who report they aren't confident enough? Thirteen. The percent of men who cite the same exact reason? Thirteen.[15]

According to McKinsey's study, men and women admit they lack confidence in equal number. Yet, we're also told that the reason more women don't break the glass ceiling is because they lack confidence. Is it any wonder that trying to close the gender gap feels like being on a treadmill to nowhere?

DOES CONFIDENCE MAKE MEN BETTER NEGOTIATORS?

Lack of confidence has also been blamed for women's failure to negotiate promotions and better wages. In their 2007 book *Women Don't Ask*, Linda Babcock and Sara Laschever argue that the wage gap in the United States is mainly due to how women approach negotiation. They support their argument with an extensive body of research showing that women initiate negotiations less often, and when they do negotiate, they consistently walk away with less than their male peers do.

One study cited found that among graduating students at Carnegie

Mellon University, eight times as many men negotiated their starting salary. Because of this, their starting salaries were 7.6 percent (or $4,000) higher than the women's in the study. The authors point out that the women's failure to negotiate put them behind from the start. Every subsequent raise will start from a lower baseline, and compounded over time, throughout their careers they'll earn dramatically less than their equally qualified male peers.[16]

If you define negotiation as one party wins and the other loses, then yes, the logical conclusion to draw from these experiments is that men are better negotiators. The problem is that it's only one *type* of negotiation. Over the past decade, the social and economic sciences have changed our understanding of *negotiation*. Its truer, more comprehensive meaning is "a discussion aimed at making an agreement." What used to be thought of as a win-lose or clash of adversaries now includes a variety of other styles. In fact, we now know that the most effective negotiations are those that seek a win-win outcome, a collaboration that results in both parties having their needs met. Win-win negotiations produce better results and preserve relationships, which are particularly important in conducting business in the long term.

In the introduction of *Women Don't Ask*, Babcock and Laschever admit that women take a collaborative approach more often than men, and that these methods can be superior to the more competitive male approach. However, they quickly dismiss these methods by saying that we live in a male-defined business world, so the female approach, although valuable, can be misinterpreted as weakness.[17] In other words, it's a man's world, so we need to discount the unique value we bring to the table, undermine our own strengths, and play by their rules.

Not everyone downplays the value of collaboration, however. In his book *Never Split the Difference: Negotiating As If Your Life Depended on It*, former FBI top hostage negotiator Chris Voss explains that there are various styles of negotiation, and each can be equally effective when done well.[18] He points to a study of American lawyer-negotiators, which found that 65 percent used a cooperative style, and when graded for effectiveness, more than 75 percent of the effective group came from the cooperative type; only 12 percent were assertive. "So if you're not assertive, don't despair," Voss wrote. "Blunt assertion is actually counterproductive most of the time."[19]

When negotiation is seen through the lens of collaboration, do women *still* fare worse? Are men simply better at reaching agreements across all situational dynamics? Dr. Hilla Dotan of Tel Aviv University's Coller School of Management and Professor Uta Herbst of Potsdam University in Germany claim that the behavioral differences between men and women in the workplace have largely been overlooked regarding research on negotiation. For example, most studies ignore the tendency for women to be more cooperative and men to be more competitive, which means most research on negotiation is studied through a very narrow lens. Taking these differences into account, Dotan and Herbst's research found that the female disadvantage in negotiations depends on the context. For example, in their experiments, women outperformed men when negotiating on behalf of friends instead of their own interests. The study concludes, "What's important for women is the sense of fighting for others, for their friends, for something bigger than themselves."[20]

Jens Mazei, while a doctoral candidate at Germany's University of Münster, came to a similar conclusion after examining fifty-one studies with a total of 10,888 participants, including businesspeople as well as graduate and undergraduate students. The researchers found that negotiation results depended on the situation and the person involved. When women negotiated on behalf of another person or knew about the bargaining range, they were better at negotiating than men.[21]

Collaborative negotiation is predicated on the ability to compromise, a skill shown to be much stronger in women. In a recent study, Hristina Nikolova, a marketing professor at Boston College, recruited college students and asked them to pick a grill they'd want to buy. Participants ranked their preference for each grill on a scale of 1 to 7. The students didn't have a strong preference for any one grill in particular.

Nikolova then split the group into pairs, with each pair selecting a grill for purchase. When the pairs were female or mixed (female/male), roughly 70 percent found a compromise with their partner, agreeing to sacrifice their first choice to better meet their partner's needs. In the male/male pairs, however, only 40 percent found middle ground.[22]

Can we pause here for a moment? That means more than half of the men refused to give in to their partner's desires for a *fake grill*. One they were never going to purchase. One they never really had a preference for anyway.

The men didn't care which grill they got but nevertheless refused to compromise on it. Doesn't that mean they just wanted to win? Doesn't it mean that their goal was to win for the sake of winning and not because they wanted the prize? More on this in later chapters.

When we define negotiation from the male point of view, as a win-lose clash between opponents, women do indeed fall short. But when we expand our understanding of what negotiation truly entails, suddenly things look different. Defining it from the female, collaborative point of view, *men* fare worse. The conventional wisdom that women lack the confidence to negotiate isn't rooted in objective truth. It's born out of a limited perspective, seeing the world through a male lens.

In other words, women aren't worse at negotiating. We only think they are because they don't do it the same way men do.

I'm not claiming that women don't lack confidence or that many of us wouldn't benefit from improving in this area. I'm saying that in the workplace, male-dominant behaviors such as arrogance, certainty, and one-upmanship are often mistaken for confidence, when they reflect the opposite. If companies reward such behavior, then it's the rewards system that is dysfunctional, not the women who are unfairly penalized.

FOUR

PUTTING THE
MEN IN *MENTOR*

*Women helped each other in ways small and large
every day, without thinking, and that was what kept
them going even when the world came up with new
and exciting ways to crush them.*

—ALYSSA COLE, *LET US DREAM*

It's often said that success in business is in large part due to relationships. This is why women are encouraged to seek mentors and pursue professional relationships with more senior people. It's why LeanIn.org created the campaign #mentorher; their website explains that people with mentors are more likely to get promoted and that women have fewer mentors than men.[1] It seems straightforward enough, a logical conclusion to draw and sensible action to take in response.

What is a mentor? In a corporate context, a mentorship is defined as a relationship where one participant has more experience, skill, and knowledge than the other. The mentor, then, is the more knowledge-able party in the relationship. "Many strong mentoring relationships provide an opportunity for both parties to learn from each other through the development of a caring and respectful partnership."[2]

Or more simply, a mentor is a kind of friend.

Have we considered how odd it is that an entire campaign was created to help women make friends? To encourage them to seek out support?

Think about it: when we become mothers, we reach out to other mom friends for advice, or we turn to one of the countless online forums dedicated to extending this kind of support. When we're hav-ing marital issues or relationship problems, what do we do? We call our friends and talk about it.

Juxtapose this with the way men typically handle the need for help and emotional support. If they're down in the dumps, do they reach out to their buddies to talk through their *feelings*? When men are sick, are they known to run to the doctor for help? When they're lost, do they stop and ask for directions?

Yet we're supposed to believe that a primary reason that men dom-inate 96 percent of the corporate C-suite is that they're better at making friends. Apparently, when trying to reach the top, men are finally okay with asking for directions on how to get there.

Compelling evidence indicates that women are better at forming connections and building stronger social networks than men.[3] For many of us, friendships are the central anchor of our lives. We take girls' trips, form book clubs, and keep in touch with childhood friends. Without the wife acting as social director, the majority of couples would be neighborhood recluses.

So why does the finesse of female friendships fail to translate into mentorship at work? Why do men seem better at building relationships and support networks in business?

––––––––

About five months into my first pregnancy, my doctor called with the news that I had gestational diabetes. It didn't endanger either me or the baby; I just had to keep my carbs under twenty grams and check my blood sugar four times a day, and the thought of giving up my thrice-daily dessert habit felt overwhelming. I hung up the phone with the doctor's office and whined about it to Carol, who was also pregnant. Not having any knowledge or advice on the matter, she suggested I join expectant_new_moms, an internal email group at Google made up of women who were pregnant or recently gave birth.

I was hesitant at first because email groups at Google were notorious for being wastelands of pedantic arguments about whether people should be allowed to not wear shoes in the café. But after many failed attempts at going cold turkey on dessert, I took Carol's advice and joined expectant_new_moms.

Two things set this email community apart from all the others at Google: it was open only to women, and it was anonymous. They'd used an engineering hack that allowed emails to be submitted and replies to be sent without anyone's name attached. Upon joining, I browsed the group's archive and was nothing short of transfixed by what I was reading. There were questions about *everything*. One woman wrote at length about her son's habit of humping the large stuffed Mickey Mouse in his crib. Others shared their fear of giving birth, tales of depression once the baby arrived, repulsion at the new shape of their bodies, and all the shame these painful feelings often evoked. There were deeply intimate matters about relationships, too, such as growing distances from partners and pregnancy hormones causing voracious sexual appetites (or a complete lack thereof).

It was the furthest thing from a cesspool of anonymous internet trolls. Women from all over the world came to each other's rescue through this invisible community of two thousand plus. Smart, professional women would sometimes spend an hour on an email thread to coach a new mom who was panicking over a lumpy breast, or would rush to another woman's aid when she forgot her key card to the office mother's room (for those who pumped breast milk). These women became an indispensable part of my survival through the two-year period when I gave birth to all three of my children. It was a community of profound, anonymous friendship and support, and the closest thing to the "sisterhood" in which I've ever taken part.

I was reminded of the new moms group while reading an article about a similarly supportive community of women in an entirely different industry: romance novels. Most people don't know that romance novels are a billion-dollar juggernaut. The size of the mystery and science-fiction/fantasy genres *combined*, romance outperforms every other category of books. More intriguing to me than the revenue numbers was the description of its author community. Unsurprisingly, the majority of writers in this genre are women, and the strength of their network is unparalleled in publishing. Sociologists Jennifer Lois at Western Washington University and Joanna Gregson at Pacific Lutheran University spent five years studying the world of romance novels. Gregson told the *New York Times*, "This community of authors is all about being egalitarian and inclusive. You see *New York Times* bestselling authors teaching brand-new authors how to write a query letter, how to get an agent." Their group emails and listservs are peppered with "all kinds of smiley face emoticons."[4]

Laurie Kahn, in her article "10 Surprising Facts About Romance

Novels," also describes the unique support between authors in the community. When she asked experienced romance writers why so many of them were willing to devote their time and attention to help newer authors, almost all of them spoke about having been a newbie to the genre and the spate of senior mentors who helped them through. Kahn describes the kind of support and mentorship:

> At a Romance Writers of America (RWA) national conference, unpublished writers are always welcome (something that does not happen at other writer conferences), and there are dozens of workshops taught by established writers about everything from plot structure and writing knife-fights, to social networking and negotiating contracts. You will see bestselling novelists sitting down for coffee with unpublished newbies, critiquing their work and giving them business advice.[5]

In the case of romance novelists and new moms at Google, women coalesced almost effortlessly around a common goal and, without personal agenda, created a support network to help one another. Considering this, it's strange that the opposite seems to happen with women helping each other climb the ladder at work.

In 2013, shortly after *Lean In* was published, Google prioritized addressing the gender gap among its female employees. A wealth of learning and development programs sprang up, and it seemed as if every other day a group of senior female leaders held a panel discussion. Women@Google became a popular employee resource group, and we formed our own chapter in New York. The day it was launched, more than one hundred women crowded into a large conference room, as a panel with three female executives addressed the crowd. The energy and optimism were palpable. Despite my usual skepticism about organized cheerleading, I couldn't help but be swept away in the excitement.

Toward the end of the session, they announced that we were going to create Lean In Circles as part of the Women@Google effort, and that everyone would be randomly assigned to a group. I left the conference room to check the list with the names of my new Lean In Circle, which included eight of us from all different parts of Google and at all levels in the organization. We met in a makeshift conference room down the hall and sat down with smiles on our faces as we went around the table, introducing ourselves. We discussed our goals, decided when our first official meeting would be, and assigned an owner to the meeting agenda. We were taking things into our own hands. We were on the precipice of real change. And it felt invigorating. For about an hour. Because that was the first and last time our Circle ever met. Despite the date scheduled in our calendars, nobody showed up for the next meeting. Some of us had work fires to put out. Others had conflicts with more important meetings. One had a personal emergency. And a handful had no reason at all.

We straight-up ghosted on our own Lean In Circle.

Three months later, at the next New York Women@Google meeting, I learned we weren't alone. This time there were about half as many of us in the audience. Seated next to our friends, we quietly admitted that *most* of our Lean In Circles had died on the vine. As far as I know, none of the Lean In Circles met more than a handful of times. Women@Google abandoned the effort and moved on to a more structured, learning style of programs that still exists today.

When I moved over to Facebook, surprisingly, it wasn't much different. At a women's leadership event in Menlo Park, a woman who worked for LeanIn.org spoke to us about why Circles are important: we need a place where women can be unapologetically ambitious, share advice, and help each other succeed. Everyone in the audience nodded, and once again, a palpable energy filled the room. *Yeah! We need to get together and help each other! Let's do this!*

And yet, as far as I know, not one person in that room ever followed up on the call to action. During my eighteen months at Facebook, I never heard of a single Circle, nor met anyone who'd participated in one. Despite being the birthplace of *Lean In*, and despite the constant encouragement, Circles were conspicuously absent.

Why did the women at Google spend hours of their time, out of their own volition, to help other moms, but quickly bow out of the Lean In Circles? Why does the romance-novel industry have such a tight community of authors who help each other succeed, but similar networks are conspicuously absent in the corporate world?

To thoroughly answer this question, we must start with a detour into the animal kingdom.

Among the many primate species, chimpanzees, our closest animal relatives, have been studied most extensively. Historically, they've served as our model for understanding evolution and human behavior. Even in the cultural mainstream, concepts of "alpha male" and "beating one's chest" are based on primatologists' observations of chimpanzees.

Chimps form male-dominated societies characterized by hierarchical power structures, with the alpha male at the top. The alpha chimp secures his position and rules his domain with physical aggression, violence, and force. For decades, scientists considered this kind of male dominance "natural," and the inevitable consequence of their larger physical size. It was believed that the females' smaller size meant they couldn't compete with, or overpower, the males in the group.

That presumption all changed in the 1990s, when renowned primatologist Amy Parish and other researchers studied another group of primates, called bonobos. Bonobos, which have a reputation for being on the randy side, are as closely related to human beings as chimps are.[6] Female bonobos are smaller than males, and the size difference is similar in proportion to that of humans. Yet bonobos are female-dominated matriarchies, with males at the very bottom. The same is true for other primate cousins, such as lemurs, macaques, and squirrel monkeys. In all cases, the males are physically larger, but the females rule.

The intriguing question is: How can females rise to dominance in the group when they're not as physically strong? Is it a David-and-Goliath situation, where the females devise scrappier ways to inflict harm, or savvier tools to kill with more precision? An even more illuminating question is: Do the females dominate by imitating male displays of power and copying the aggressive tactics?

In short, the answer is no. In bonobo societies, the females don't dominate by acting more like males, and they don't garner power in any way resembling that of the alpha chimp. In these primate matriarchies, power is defined not by physicality and aggression but by relationships.[7]

One-on-one, a male bonobo can overpower a female, but when females unite as a group, a male has no shot. Therefore, it is the relationships the females form that protect them from being overpowered, and the strength of these female connections inevitably controls the group's males. If the male bonobos banded together, they could easily overpower the females. But they don't, because male bonobos have relatively weak bonds with each other.

The idea of strength in numbers holds up on both sides: in male-dominated primate groups, like chimpanzees, bonds between females are weak, and those between males are strong. As it turns out, the strength of connection within gender, rather than physical size and strength, predicts dominance.

While male-dominant chimp societies are characterized by aggression and physical force, female-dominant bonobo societies are better described as a commune of horny hippies. In a bonobo matriarchy, sex is the substitute for aggression.[8] Although females can and do become violent against the males in the group, overall, they're less aggressive, and they rely more on the power of cooperation than on physical force.

According to Amy Parish, the natural solidarity of female bonobos gives them power. Of their relationships Parish said, "Females had these really intense and enduring friendships with each other, and that was even more rare among mammals." Males, on the other hand, had weaker bonds. "The males can be friendly. They have sex with each other. But it's nothing like the intensity or the scope that we see in the females." She also noted that these relationships translate to power in bonobo society, saying, "Females can be in charge. They can control the resources. They don't need to go through males to get them. They don't have to be subjected to sexual violence."[9]

In the primate world, males and females build and exert power in very different ways: relationship and connection versus aggression and physical force. Although the analogy to humans isn't precise, this information provides important takeaways about the concept of power; namely, that in our culture we've defined power against a male template. We conceptualize it in a narrow way, through a male lens, and have failed to see the larger picture. A female-dominated world wouldn't entail a switch in the ratio of male to female CEOs and politicians. Our attempts to amass power in the same way as men is misguided, not only because this strategy has failed, but because it undermines the power we already have.

I once worked for a great guy at Google named Scott. One of his best qualities was that he understood his employees as individuals. He knew each of our unique strengths and the areas where we needed to grow. Unlike many other performance reviews I've received in my career, Scott's were genuinely insightful, and his advice was spot-on. I still have a copy of one of his old reviews, and one sentence in particular has always stuck with me. It provided guidance on how to improve my client relationships:

> *Transition from "we love Marissa" to "we love*
> *Marissa and she helps us grow our business."*

At the time, my clients were the advertising executives across different ad agencies in New York. I wasn't a salesperson, as I wasn't selling them anything. Rather, my job was to be the friendly face of Google, so they would consider us a great, helpful partner rather than a competitor (which made it easier for the sales teams to close deals). The whole point of my job was to get my clients to love me. So when they did, and Scott felt it wasn't enough, I was confused.

When I asked Scott about it in our formal review, he explained that our clients' love for me was great and all, but on its own it held no currency. Relationships, he told me, were only as good as what they bring you, and mine weren't bringing in anything tangible.

I understood Scott's point, and I didn't think he was necessarily wrong. But it has always been hard for me to think about my relationships in that way. For me, the relationships I build hold currency in that I derive enjoyment from the feelings of connection they bring. Trying to leverage them for some business advantage feels compromising, threatening the strong connections I take great care to build.

In this scenario, neither way is right or wrong. Scott and I simply don't experience relationships the same way. For people like me, connection to others is its own reward. For people like Scott, relationships for their own sake aren't as rewarding, and these types of people derive less enjoyment from connection. It's not necessarily that the Scotts of the world see all their relationships as a means to an end. It's that they're more willing to put those relationships at risk to gain something in return. It's not a binary good/bad, black/white kind of thing, where you're either a hippie or Gordon Gekko. It's a continuum with many shades, on which you index more toward one side than the other in most, but not all, parts of your life.

Let's overgeneralize for a moment and pretend that Scott represents all men, and I represent all women. I would be better than Scott at nurturing a strong circle of girlfriends in my personal life, and Scott would be better at doing so in business, where these relationships yield more tangible outcomes. When men like Scott select "mentors" and form boys' clubs at work, the outcome can be defined more as an *alliance* than as a close circle of friendship. Men like competition, and the corporate world is a political cesspool, where trading favors can help you succeed. If you're like me, however, doing this is uncomfortable because it threatens the connection and trust in the relationship.

Neither I nor Scott are superior to each other in this regard. We simply derive different emotional rewards from our relationships. The problem is that most corporations run a zero-sum competition, and that means the Scotts of the world will fare better. Not because they're more suited for success, but because they're more suited for competition. If you change the rules of the game, and success is predicated on a win-win dynamic, people like me, who are more suited for collaboration and more adept at building relationships, will rise to the top.

The inherent power in female relationships is what we see

manifested in the romance-novel industry, the new moms group, and the female-dominated matriarchies of the animal world.

In light of this, we can better understand why women easily come together in certain areas and fail to do so in others. Amassing power and success in the corporate world comes at the expense of one's relationships. Because of its nature as a competitive, zero-sum game, for someone to succeed, another person must lose. At Facebook and Google, employees are graded on a curve. No two people on the same team can be equally amazing or equally terrible; you must be more amazing or more terrible than your closest peer. Similarly, to "win" a promotion, your peer must lose. Spots are scarce, and competition is fierce, intensifying the higher on the ladder you climb. This competitive, win-lose system discourages cooperative behavior and destroys the fabric of female relationships.

Romance novelists are in a win-win environment. The genre's readership is in the millions, and they buy more books all the time. If they love one author, and a new one comes on the scene, a reader doesn't have to choose between them when buying a book. She can buy both. Therefore, if one author helps another succeed, this doesn't threaten her livelihood.

The threat to relationships isn't just an abstract concept, as evidence shows that women derive much of their satisfaction in life from relationships and connection.[10] When given the opportunity to forge these connections for mutual gain, women are unstoppable. But the zero-sum competitive games of the corporate world pit us against each other, and in this competition to nowhere, our relationships are the first casualties.

For women, competitions erode more than just relationships; they reduce our creativity and work performance. Researchers from Washington University in Saint Louis studied the strengths and weaknesses of men and women working in groups. Their results show that women are more creative in groups built on collaboration. Throw a competitive component into the picture, and they begin to falter. Men are the exact opposite. As the study's authors state, "If teams work side by side, women tend to perform better and even outperform men— they're more creative. As soon as you add the element of competition though, the picture changes. Men under those circumstances gel together. They become more interdependent and more collaborative, and women just do the opposite."[11]

The effects of competitive versus cooperative systems will be addressed in more detail in chapter 7. For now, though, the point is this: women derive satisfaction, reward, and power from building and sustaining relationships. The win-lose games of a corporate hierarchy erode the very thing that makes women strong. Corporations are structured as competitions not because they're superior to all other arrangements, but because they were created by men, through a male worldview, at a time when virtually no women were in the workforce. Women are under the microscope for their failure to play by men's rules, instead of everyone stepping back and recognizing that the world has changed, and the rules are no longer working.

SCHOOL VS. WORK

The universe makes sure there isn't much of a link between job performance in the corporate world and outcomes.

—SCOTT ADAMS, *HOW TO FAIL AT ALMOST EVERYTHING AND STILL WIN BIG*

In 2017, women earned 57 percent of all undergraduate degrees. In the same year, they held the majority of both masters (59.2 percent) and doctoral degrees (53.5 percent) for first-time graduate students.[1] Their majority position isn't the result of a recent trend, nor was it built slowly over time. *Every year* since 1982, more bachelor's degrees have been conferred on women than on men. Female dominance of academia invites an intriguing question: Why doesn't this dominance continue after graduation?

Once again, conventional wisdom points us to cultural conditioning. Girls are taught to be compliant and follow the rules, which works well in academia but not in the corporate world. For example, in her seminal book, *Nice Girls Don't Get the Corner Office*, Lois Frankel explains: "From early childhood, girls are taught that their well-being and ultimate success are contingent upon acting in certain stereotypical ways, such as being polite, soft-spoken, compliant, and relationship-oriented."[2]

Linda Babcock and Sara Laschever's book, *Women Don't Ask*, also supports this theory, telling us that girls are conditioned to be deferential and to expect little in return, whereas boys are conditioned to make things happen and to expect money as a result.[3] I suppose the former helps you succeed in school, but the latter makes you a CEO.

In *The Confidence Code*, Kay and Shipman get even more specific, pointing blame at schools themselves. According to their book, the classrooms of our youth are the training grounds where we first learn that "good girls" stay quiet, look neat, and appear perfect. As a result, they breed women who, as adults, avoid risks, fear mistakes, and remain silent.[4]

Shipman tells us she's fighting this tide in her own family by encouraging her daughter Della to speak up and participate more often in class. When Della came home from school one day and said she raises her hand all the time now, "even when [she doesn't] have anything important to say," Shipman was *ecstatic*.[5] I guess her lessons on the virtue of being a windbag were paying off.

Hopefully, you get the crux of the argument by now: school favors compliant behavior, and women are sheep. Or schools turn them into sheep. To succeed, women need to be reconditioned into wolves. Or something like that.

The argument has several facets, but the one we'll unpack in this chapter is this question: Are behaviors such as politeness, obedience, and being relationship oriented really the keys to female success in school but their undoing in business?

―――――

During my sophomore year of college, I took a really boring course called Business Law, along with my roommate, Jodi. I never actually went to class, but I know it was boring because it had both "business" and "law" in the title. Jodi was a bright and conscientious student who attended every class, took detailed notes on each lecture, and kept up with the required weekly reading. Like Jodi, I wanted to do well in the class, but I lacked the certain kind of discipline known as "not being lazy."

The morning before our midterm, Jodi stopped by my room on her way to the library. I still hadn't read a single page of the course material, so being the positive and supportive friend that she is, she stuck her head inside the door and said, "There's no way you can read all this by tomorrow. You're going to fail the test."

"I'm pulling an all-nighter."

"Good luck with that!"

"I'm going to get a better grade than you."

"Ha! Let's put fifty bucks on it."

Since fifty dollars was the price of ~~an ounce of weed~~ an important textbook I needed, I took her up on the bet. I studied from 3:00 p.m. that afternoon till our midterm at 3:00 p.m. the next day, and sat right next to Jodi for the exam.

Our scores became available a couple of days later through the class website. Sitting on my bed, I held my breath and logged in to see my grade: 94 percent. I thought I was hallucinating. Jodi appeared at the door of my room a few minutes later, smirking.

"Ninety-twooooo, beyotch!"

"I got a 94. I think that's higher than a 92, but I'm not sure because I haven't attended any of my calculus classes this semester."

"Shut. Up."

I smirked.

"I hate you."

"But I lovvvvve you."

"Can I at least have some of the weed?"

"Of course."

If our business law professor had graded us the way our managers grade us in the corporate world, Jodi would be an A student, and I'd be the corporate dropout I am right now. Her behavior was what teachers wanted and expected. She followed their rules like the conscientious student that she is. On the other hand, I didn't even know what my teacher looked like or where the class was held on campus. If he'd had the power to fail me, my professor would've pulled the trigger without hesitation. Even though I met the goal of learning the material, my way of doing it probably would've been *insulting*. It showed a disregard for the rules and minimized his role in the learning process.

But on the midterm, I got ninety-four out of one hundred answers correct. My score was a 94 whether I had studied for five weeks or five minutes. I got an A regardless of whether I was a quiet, obedient nice girl or a brash, aggressive asshole.

In academia, the objectivity of grades means that success is judged on results, not on how well one behaves. This seems to contradict the theory put forth by the books in the beginning of this chapter. But before we pass a verdict, let's look at how things work in the corporate world, where we don't have exams and scores to judge our performance.

Without these objective measures, how do managers decide which employees get an A grade?

CALIBRATION OF DOOM

"He is a jerk! A total jerk!"

The head of a large man named Vic fills the screen on the video conference, and my friend Taylor is on the brink of a total breakdown. The "total jerk" in question is Alex, and Taylor is his manager. Vic and Taylor each manage their own teams of ten people, and only one promotion is available across all twenty of them. Taylor believes the spot should go to Alex, but Vic clearly thinks Alex is a total jerk. At least that's what he needs to convince the calibration committee of, so the spot can go to the person he wants for the promotion, Brian. The bigger commotion he makes about Alex being not only bad at his job, but also bad as a person, the more likely Vic will win this fight.

Trapped in a stuffy conference room alongside eight other managers, Taylor and Vic continue arguing for twenty-five minutes. Nobody can leave until a decision is reached.

Welcome to calibrations.

Calibration meetings happen twice a year in conference rooms across Google and Facebook. Just like every Rosh Hashanah, God decides the fate of Jews everywhere, and we Jews pray for a good verdict, calibrations are the altar on which employee worth is judged and fates are sealed.

In calibration meetings, promotions and performance scores are decided by a group of managers for a given team. While your direct manager attends, the others in the room usually have little to no clue who you are, let alone the quality of your work. Some of you may be wondering why employees are graded by a committee like this. Shouldn't your manager just give you a grade based on how well you did?

Please, come take a seat and let me tell you a little story about what really goes on in the world's most progressive tech companies.

The reason calibration meetings exist, and a group of managers have to fight for scores, is because those scores must fit a specific distribution. A certain number of employees must end up in the top, middle, and lower buckets of the distribution. In a given department, only so many people can be good, a certain number must be bad, and most are required to fall somewhere in the middle.

Generally, it looks something like this:

Performance of Employees

Fights ensue not just over who gets the scarce promotional spot, but also over how each person on the team gets scored. If too many people are in the "good" bucket, managers have to collectively decide who will get pushed down to "fairly good." In these tense moments, when an employee's fate is being decided, his or her competence, talent, and effort hardly matter. The better scores go to the manager who's better at getting his or her way. Vic won in the fight against Taylor that day, and Brian got promoted, not because Brian deserved it more than

Alex, but because Vic was so aggressive and intolerable that he wore everyone down until they gave in.

The story of Vic and Taylor serves as an example of how performance is rated in the absence of objective measures, like grades. The process has little to do with the merits of your work; so many unrelated factors go into the decision. For example, if you have a manager who doesn't represent your work well or doesn't fight hard enough for you in the calibration meeting, his or her failure becomes the biggest influence on your promotion.

An important clarification: grading on a curve in school is different from the forced distribution described above. In school, teachers make the curve *after* the students take the test—for example, if the highest grade is a 90, then they'll start the curve there and retrofit the other grades. At Google and Facebook, the distribution is set before any work is done, and performance is then forced to fit into it. The only thing these distributions have in common is the word used to describe them. In school, curves are used as a tool for fairness; if the test was too hard, and the highest score was an 85, it makes some logical sense to set that as the benchmark for an A grade. In contrast, a forced distribution is completely arbitrary. If everyone scores 100 percent, the forced distribution means you have to decide who gets the As and who gets the Bs. Even if everyone scored perfectly, theoretically, managers would still need to decide who fails. It's just how the distribution works.

Calibrations are where people get slotted into the distribution, but it's important to understand that managers show up to the meetings with people's scores already in mind. Their ability to fight for the scores is just one piece of the puzzle. How do they come up with them in the first place?

———

Big companies have lots of people around, doing lots of different things, making it hard to draw clear lines between the work people do and its impact on the business. High performance is hard to detect, and low performance is easy to cover up. To explain how this environment affects performance ratings and determines the winners, let's do a thought experiment.

For the NBA draft, basketball players are ranked by experts who use data on their past performance and observations from the court. The data is concrete, objective, and neatly benchmarked; players can be compared with each other on an apples-to-apples basis. The observations are direct; the experts can watch players in action.

Now imagine a scenario in which the panel of experts were not allowed to observe the players on the court and had very little on their performance data. What they *did* have was essentially worthless because it was inconsistent across players; some had points per game, while others had numbers of assists.

To decide the rankings, each player stands before the panel, describes his effort, and summarizes his performance. If players want to be ranked highly, they have to make a case for it, demonstrating why they're the most talented and deserve to be at the top.

If we consider school to be loosely analogous to the first scenario and the corporate world to the second, we can ask a few helpful questions. Which system would be better at surfacing talent? In the second scenario, which basketball players would we assume get the high rankings? If the experts couldn't identify actual talent, what would be used as its proxy? If we had to advise the basketball players on winning a top spot, wouldn't we tell them to argue their case for being number one, even if they weren't technically that good? Wouldn't it help if they exaggerated their talent and made the other players seem inferior by comparison? Shouldn't they seek out the judges as often as they can, kiss their asses a little, and make sure they're always standing in front of the crowd, where they can be seen and heard?

A real-world example of this can be seen in the realm of orchestras, which over the past several decades have changed the way they hire musicians. In the late 1970s, women made up fewer than 5 percent of the United States' top orchestra musicians. By 1997 that number had increased to 25 percent, and today some orchestras are above 30 percent.[6] Considering that we're still hovering around 4 percent of female CEOs after decades of effort, the leap in female orchestra musicians appears remarkable.

So how did orchestras do it? They put up a screen, so the people evaluating the performance couldn't see the performer. Their ratings were based purely on the music produced instead of the person producing it. As with grades, when performance is judged objectively, women fare remarkably better.

In school, good grades are based on competence and effort. At work, success is predicated on *acting* competent and *making a big show of your effort*. It's no coincidence that self-aggrandizement and bravado, largely the domain of men, are rewarded more often.

Clarifying the problem in this way makes it a lot easier to see the solutions. Are we better off trying to change women into men, or should we try to define success more clearly and objectively?

Although the latter is obviously more practical, it's a highly unlikely solution, not because it wouldn't work (it probably would), but because having measurable targets makes managers accountable for hitting them. Managers don't like that.

On the marketing team at Facebook, we were responsible for writing the sales pitches for our advertising products. Writing stories that sell is *really* hard. Like most people, my teammates sucked at it. But it's also a critical part of selling, so the sales teams were frustrated that marketing kept handing them shitty PowerPoints that were boring and full of jargon, and that made their job harder. When Robert, the head of US sales, began complaining loudly about it, the marketing executives finally decided that something had to be done.

Creating an entirely new library of stories and pitch decks became priority number one, and Sonia, my direct boss, who also was new to the company, was chosen to head up the highly visible and politically fraught project.

Over the next month, in sales meetings across the company, Sonia publicly committed to a solution. She promised the salespeople that the marketing team would deliver a brand-new library of compelling stories and pitch decks by the end of the year. It was January at this point. She had fewer than twelve months to save the marketing team's reputation, not to mention her own.

This kind of storytelling was exactly what I did in my final two years at Google. I wrote pitch decks for YouTube, Facebook's biggest competitor, and I traveled around the United States and Europe, teaching our salespeople how to deliver the pitches. While storytelling wasn't a strength for the majority of people on our team, it was the one thing I knew how to do well, and I had a successful track record of delivering effective pitch decks to the sales teams at Google. I felt uniquely suited to help Sonia write new ones and build out the library.

Believing this was a win-win for both of us, I approached Sonia and explained how I could help with the project. I laid out a plan that would allow me to create the story library while keeping up with my day job. And on top of that, I'd be able to have the first draft of stories done in a month and the final versions in just eight weeks.

Sonia nodded along and thanked me for the suggestion, but said she needed some time to think about it.

I learned of her decision a few weeks later, when she presented her plan at the national sales meeting. Sonia hired a team of consultants from Accenture, who would rewrite all of the sales stories and build a better archive. They'd have everything done by December 31. It was now February. The salespeople seemed pleased.

Later on, Sonia shared the finer details of the plan with a smaller group of us in marketing. Of the eight consultants we hired, only one had ever worked in digital advertising. They knew virtually nothing about our products, our market, our competition, or our salespeople's needs. Over the coming year, we'd act as their stewards in the process, while they wrote the stories and designed the slides. It would be nine months before sales could see a first draft. The total cost of the project? A quarter of a million dollars.

As far as I know, Sonia never mentioned my original proposal, and I didn't ask. We never spoke of it again.

Although having me write the stories would have saved Facebook $250,000 and would have taken two months instead of ten, I now see why it would have been a bad move for Sonia. Imagine if she stood up in front of hundreds of salespeople and announced that she was going to solve their biggest sales challenge by . . . putting someone from her team on the job in that person's spare time. It doesn't project the right image, especially for a senior manager whose first assignment at the company was such a high-visibility affair. It sounds way more impressive to announce that we were laying out a quarter of a million dollars and devoting an entire year to it. This *really* makes an impression on the audience: marketing is *very serious* about this, and their commitment makes them an invaluable partner to sales.

Sonia's visibility increased in direct proportion to the size and magnitude of the project. Hiring Accenture was also a smart move; it's a well-known, prestigious firm. Associating herself with their brand made the project, and thus her reputation, appear more distinguished.

Sonia positioned herself as a hero in her first month at Facebook, and it solidified her image as a leader who's willing to put a stake in the ground to get things done.

But what would have happened if Sonia's success had been defined up front? What if the marketing executives planned to survey sales about the utility of the new sales decks, and set clear targets to hit? And what if efficiency metrics were put into place? That is, how much time and money it would take, along with trade-offs on quality? If success had been defined in terms of what's best for the business, not for her reputation, the situation may have proceeded differently.

Without clear goals to assess how well Sonia solved the problem, what mattered was how important she *looked* while solving it.

Another common example of this phenomenon is what's known as the "company reorg." It seems that every time a new leader joins an organization, or if the current one needs to prove he or she has a plan to turn things around, a reorg is inevitable. Reorgs usually start off with a vague announcement from the leadership team: an ominous warning about an upcoming structural change to the organization. The lack of clarity, coupled with news of impending change, creates palpable fear among employees, who suddenly are unsure about their job security. Some people see the reorg as an opportunity to score a better, more senior role, while others see it as a need to justify their current positions. Either way, a frenzy of posturing, secret meetings, and politicking erupts, as people vie for more information and secure their spots in the new org structure. From the outside or from above, this sudden movement, the shuffling of the existing order, looks like progress. Appearing as someone who gets things done, the leader of a reorg gets an instant shot of credibility and a boost to his or her image. And by harboring information and creating fear, they only grow more powerful and important in the company.

The impact of a reorg is almost never assessed after the fact. Nobody ever knows, or seems to care, whether it was a good decision or how it impacted the bottom line. The lack of accountability makes reorgs one of the sharpest and most often used tools in the toolbox of corporate leadership. It solidifies a leader's reputation and increases his or her power, regardless of how things turn out. Reorgs are a no-lose proposition for a corporate executive, and almost always a no-win for everyone else.

In cases like Sonia's story project, or with any company reorg, success metrics would instill much needed accountability. So why are they seldom put in place? Because objectivity and accountability are just plain scary to most people. If Sonia had to get ten stories done in three months with a 7+ rating from sales, success or failure is clear-cut. Imagine the fear of missing the target. Would she be seen as incompetent? Would she be fired? Given a second chance? The same goes for corporate leadership amid a reorg. Keeping the objectives vague and success ambiguous is the much safer route. It preserves power among the powerful. And it's nothing unique—it's what everyone does across all of corporate America, every day, across every industry. Accountability is scary when your livelihood depends on it. And we're only human.

These challenges to objectivity are solvable, only if we recognize the part they play in the gender gap. The bigger problem than gender bias is *system* bias. The way we judge competence and evaluate good work is broken and biased toward traits that are more common among men.

In contrast, schools grade on outcome, not behavior. The objectivity of grades is the ultimate equalizer. And *that* is why women dominate academia. The lack of objectivity in the corporate world results in a dysfunctional and biased system that rewards male-dominant behaviors. They are proxies for competence that don't correlate to competence. Right now, instead of trying to design better performance systems, we try to design better women.

SIX

#SORRYNOTSORRY

When you grow up as a girl, it is like there are faint chalk lines traced approximately three inches around your entire body at all times, drawn by society and often religion and family and particularly other women, who somehow feel invested in how you behave, as if your actions reflect directly on all womanhood.

—M. E. Thomas, *Confessions of a Sociopath*

Earlier this year, I was picking up my seven-year-old daughter from her friend's birthday party when I noticed one of her classmate's T-shirts, which read:

I'm a ~~princess~~
I'm a smart, talented girl

I'm all for smart, talented girls, but the shirt annoyed me. My daughter loves to put on makeup and dance around the house, pretending to be a princess. She loves princess dresses and princess movies. Her bedroom wall is plastered with princess posters; it's a virtual shrine to all things royal. Does her predilection for princesses come at the expense of her being smart and talented? Why do we consider it bad for little girls to like girly things?

The T-shirt was emblematic of a new trend in the modern campaign for gender equality: girl shaming.

Most popular feminist books, especially ones on closing the gender gap, share a similar formula. They start out by painting culture as a kind of invisible boogeyman conditioning young girls to act within stereotype: comply; be humble, polite, and reserved; and so on. They argue that women continue these behaviors as adults, which limits their success in ways of which they're not even aware.

Once the stage is set, the author swoops in as the hero who will save us from our false selves. To reverse our conditioning, they urge us to rebel against the template of female behavior. Since society punishes us for being aggressive, we need to fight back by being *more* aggressive. Because we're expected to sit down and be quiet, we should stand up and be loud. We need to renounce our icky *girl* selves if we want to seize our rightful place at the table. These actions are also painted as heroic, a rising up against the forces that try to keep us down.

I doubt any of the authors in this genre think of their narratives in this way. In fact, they all begin their books by preempting the accusation. Somewhere in the introduction, each tries to clarify her aim; she's not trying to fix women and not suggesting there's anything wrong with us. But in all cases, these authors spend the remaining two-hundred-plus pages doing exactly that. Perhaps their intentions are noble, but the authors are clearly disappointed (and in some cases nearly disgusted) by the behavior of women at large.

I also understand where their sentiment comes from. Historically, women were enslaved by stereotypes that formed the real-world boundaries on what was considered acceptable behavior for a woman. And even now, acting against stereotype is often met with scorn. It makes sense that part of our desire to transcend the shackles of sub-jugation would include a rebellion against stereotypes. But the way these authors go about it is completely misguided. Now we're punishing women for acting within the stereotype, the same way we punish those who act outside of it. The ultimate goal is freedom: freedom to act in a way that's authentic to who you are, not as it's prescribed. A prescription to behave outside the lines is still a prescription on how to behave.

There is also an important distinction between the girl-shaming books covered in this chapter and those in the personal growth/self-help genre. The latter books are about improving yourself and your quality of life. The former are about fixing female deficiencies by teaching women how to become more like men.

In 2008, Linda Babcock came to Google and gave a talk about her book *Ask for It: How Women Can Use the Power of Negotiation to Get What They Really Want.*

I'd always been intrigued by the topic of gender, so I was excited for Babcock's talk. In her lecture, she explained that due to our cultural conditioning, women don't ask for what they want as often as men, and we pay a steep price for this timidity; our failure to negotiate is the primary driver of the country's wage and gender gap. She closed with an overview of her four-part framework aimed at helping women speak up and ask for what we want.

I found her talk inspiring but wasn't clear about a couple of things in her research. So, during the Q&A session, I stepped up to the mic with my question. I asked if women go for raises less often because they value other things more highly. I was curious whether the desire for flexibility or part-time work affected how often they ask for raises.

Babcock seemed to tighten up as I spoke. When I finished, she took a long, slow, exaggerated breath, as if she were trying to calm herself, so she could figure out how to answer the stupidest f*cking question she'd ever heard in her life. With a smirk, she finally said, "You're asking me . . . if women don't like money?"

This got a chuckle from the audience, which seemed to please Babcock. They all agreed I was an idiot. I wanted to crawl under the chair.

I replied into the mic: "Bitch, didn't you just write a book encouraging women to *ask* shit? So why you gotta make me feel like an asshole?"

Oh wait, no. That's what I said to her in my head that night as I replayed the scene for the hundredth time before falling asleep. In reality, I fumbled through a half apology, half clarification. "Sorry . . . no . . . I obviously know women like money. I was just wondering if women asked for other stuff more often? Like . . . maybe they'd rather forgo a raise in order to work from home or something."

Babcock moved from public humiliation to outright dismissal.

"I'm not getting into a nature-versus-nurture debate right now, if that's what you're trying to do. Next question. Thank you."

It seems only fitting to start our review of girl shaming with the book that marked my unwitting entrée into the world of gender politics, Linda Babcock and Sara Laschever's *Women Don't Ask*.

Women Don't Ask tells us that women rarely ask for what they want and deserve in both their personal and professional lives. A lack of self-assertion in this regard can have significant consequences; failure to negotiate salary can cost a woman more than half a million dollars over her career.[1] In contrast, men are four times more likely to ask for a raise, even when women are equally qualified. The book then teaches you how to be a better negotiator, by overcoming all the ways that you act like a woman.

The authors clarify their aims early. Their book isn't about some inexplicable female failing that can easily be corrected. It is not about ways that women need to fix themselves. No, these authors have a loftier goal: inspiring everyone . . . to think differently about how women can and should behave.[2]

Hmm. So they're not trying to fix us or change our behavior; they just want us to behave *differently*. Got it.

Before attempting to understand *why* women don't ask, I wanted to know: Is it true that they don't? Do we really ask for raises less often than men do? In most books of this nature, the authors weave a tapestry of facts, research, and opinion, and by the end, they've answered these questions and convinced us of their conclusion. But Babcock and Laschever spare us this tradition. The very first sentence of the preface simply reads, "Women don't ask." The second, third, and fourth sentences pile it on: "They don't ask for raises and promotions and better job opportunities. They don't ask for recognition for the good work they do. They don't ask for more help at home."[3]

I couldn't help reading their tone as, "*Women don't ask for shit, okay?! Don't even dare question if it's true, because it's true. Women don't get what they want in this world, and we're gonna help them, okay?*"

Okay.

The book's introduction is the first place where we learn of the research supporting the claim that women don't ask. The first study, conducted by Babcock herself, looks at the starting salaries of students who graduated from Carnegie Mellon. As we discussed in chapter 3, the men in the group started with salaries that were, on average, 7.6 percent higher than those of the women. Only 7 percent of the female students had negotiated versus 57 percent of the men.[4] Seems like solid evidence of their point, conflict of interest notwithstanding.

The second study, also conducted by Babcock, along with two colleagues, included a game of Boggle and a three-dollar reward. After several rounds of the game, the experimenter handed the participant the three dollars and said, "Here's three dollars. Is three dollars okay?" If participants asked for more, they were handed ten dollars instead. I'm sure you can guess where this is going. Yup. Nine times as many men asked for more money.[5] So, a game from the 1970s, played for pocket change, is the microcosm of reality upon which we draw sweeping conclusions about women's timidity.

Since the premise of their book was largely supported with the author's own studies, I thought it was worth exploring what the latest research tells us about women's propensity (or lack thereof) to ask for what they want.

McKinsey and LeanIn.org's *Women in the Workplace* has become a popular reference for the latest research on the gender gap, so I started with their 2017 report. To my surprise and delight, it included an entire section on the different rates at which men and women ask for promotions. But the first snippet from the headline article caught me off guard: "Women are just as interested in being promoted as men, and they ask for promotions at comparable rates."[6]

Ruh-roh. Could it be . . . ?

I kept reading.

It got worse.

"Senior-level *women ask for promotions more often* than senior-level men."[7]

Did McKinsey and LeanIn.org just overturn the entire premise of *Women Don't Ask*? Yes. I believe they did.

Okay, guys, I have to be honest. My plan was to do additional research, then continue with a thorough analysis of Babcock and Laschever's entire book. But based on the fact that women *do* ask, and in some cases ask *more* than men, I didn't see the point. And besides, I was chomping at the bit to get to this next book.

Nice Girls Don't Get the Corner Office, by Lois Frankel, was kind of the *Lean In* of the early aughts. A seminal book on modern feminism and probably the first of its kind, it was heralded as the definitive guide for women to get ahead. Ten years later, in 2014, an updated version of the book was published, this time titled: *Nice Girls Still Don't Get the Corner Office*.

Frankel says she wrote the new edition of the book because there's still more work to do. Or more precisely, because her first book about how girls can get the corner office failed to get girls corner offices.[8] That's not just my snarky opinion, by the way. Frankel says it herself in the introduction, not to mention that it says so right there in the book's title (*Nice Girls* Still *Don't . . .*).

Since nothing has changed since Frankel's book, one might expect her new version to explore where we've gone wrong. A reexamination of her assumptions seems like a useful starting point, or perhaps sharing feedback from readers on what challenges persist despite acting on her advice. But alas, this wasn't the direction Frankel was apt to take. Thoughtful deliberation wasn't necessary because she already knows why the first book didn't work: readers didn't know how to act on her advice. So, in the new version, she fixes the problem by spelling everything out so clearly that even a woman can understand it!

The overall goal of *Nice Girls* is to teach women how to succeed, despite being ~~weak and stupid~~ nice. Whereas *The Confidence Code* and *Women Don't Ask* home in on just *one* of our behavioral failings, Frankel was way more ambitious. *Nice Girls Still Don't Get the Corner*

Office covers 133 "typical mistakes women make due to their social-ization."[9] *One hundred thirty-three* ways we screw things up without even knowing it.

Like Babcock and Laschever, Frankel softens the blow of her mes-sage by reminding us that it's not our fault. We're not failures because we're "stupid or incompetent." We're simply "acting in ways consistent with [our] socialization. . . . Beyond girlhood, no one ever *tells* us that acting differently is an option—and so we don't. . . . Unaware of the alternatives, we often fail to develop a repertoire of woman-appropriate behaviors."[10]

It's not that women are stupid—we just *act* stupid. Got it.

She also defends against the accusation that she's advising us to be more like men. It's not true, she says. Being "nice is necessary for suc-cess; it's simply not sufficient." We must also develop "complementary behaviors."[11] Sooooo, to be successful, we should still be nice, but also be like men. Got it.

The formula so far:

✓ Culture is the source of all female failings.
✓ Behaving like a woman is career suicide.

Taking us further down her chain of logic and condescension, Frankel tells us that our biggest problem isn't that we were taught to be nice little girls. It's that women wind up acting like little girls, even after they've grown up. She says that compared to boys, girls are likable. They are cuddly and sweet and don't ask for much. They are like *pets*. Yes, ladies and gentlemen. It's right there on page 3. Girls are like *pets*.

To recap Frankel's argument thus far: Girls are programmed to be nice, which is at the root of all of our incompetence. Even as adult women, we act like chihuahuas, and since we were too dumb to listen to her the first time, Frankel had to spell it out for us with *133* shitty behaviors that make us total failures.

Well, I certainly feel all empowered now, don't you?

But of course, there's no need to worry. Frankel generously provides detailed instructions for correcting the error of our ways. And she knows they work, because her clients have told her so.

- ✓ Culture is the source of all female failings.
- ✓ Behaving like a woman is career suicide.
- ✓ Author swoops in to save us from ourselves.

I have to admit, I didn't expect to find much substance as I read through the list of nice-girl mistakes in this book. But cracking open chapter 2 was like a smack in the face. I was guilty of the very first one on the list, and it's exactly what precipitated my demise at work. To Frankel's credit, she clearly understands the corporate world. Mistake #1 is "Pretending It Isn't a Game."[12]

Frankel starts this chapter with a story about a women's softball game in college. Toward the end of the game, one of the girls smacked the ball over the fence, scoring a home run for the first time in her college career. As she ran to base, she tore a ligament in her leg and had to stop. Being a senior at the end of softball season, it was her last chance at a home run, but she couldn't walk or touch the bases; it was all about to slip through her fingers forever. Players on the opposing team understood the significance of what was happening, swooped her up, and carried her across the field to each base. The injured girl completed the season having scored her first and only home run of her college career.[13]

You may be thinking that this is a touching story that exemplifies the best of women and their propensity to care for others. At least that's what I was thinking. But Frankel didn't begin with this story to celebrate the sisterhood's more nurturing and benevolent aspects. No, it was meant to underscore what she sees as a uniquely female phenomenon: we're too nice, and that's why we never win. Winning, she says, is what moves us from nice girl to successful woman. The girls on the opposing team did a nice thing, but winning is more important. By helping the injured girl make her dreams come true, the opposing team compromised their chance of winning the game.[14] And that makes them losers. In life.

She asks us if we think men would have done the same thing in this situation. No. No they wouldn't. Instead, she refers to something a male executive at Nestlé once told her: "When a man's friend wins, a little piece of him dies."[15] Frankel believes that this is the attitude women must adopt if we want to stop being losers.

Frankel also points out that work is a game with winners and losers, but women approach it as they would a picnic, a place where everyone comes together and plays nicely. She points to our desire for win-win outcomes as the reason we end up being losers.[16]

Oh lord, where do I even begin? Yes, the corporate world *is* a game, and it *is* mostly a win-lose proposition. On that, Frankel and I can agree. But if women prefer win-win scenarios, wouldn't it make sense for companies to build rewards for collaboration and design projects that depend on cooperative effort? For all the recent business and management literature extolling the virtues of collaboration and the need for effective teamwork, it seems as though people who strive for win-wins would be assets to an organization, no? Competition and win-lose games aren't the only way to organize employees and design reward systems. It is the way companies were originally organized, by men, in the industrial age. We just believe that's the only option because that's all we know.

Other gems on the list:[17]

- Mistake 10: Being Naive
  - If you're "the only one in the room who disagrees with the consensus . . . an alarm should go off that you're being naive."[18]
- Mistake 14: Being the Conscience
  - "The terrorist attacks of September 11 and the spate of shady corporate financial dealings in the early 2000s gave us three extreme examples of women being the conscience—only to find they were ignored, stonewalled, or crucified."[19]
- Mistake 25: Needing to Be Liked
- Mistake 30: Telling the Whole Truth and Nothing but the Truth
- Mistake 36: Decorating Your Office Like Your Living Room [side note: WTF]
- Mistake 37: Feeding Others
  - "We don't ascribe a sense of impact or import to people who feed others."[20] [Yes. She's talking about actual food.]
  - "The act of feeding is equated with nourishing, and nourishing is *definitely* a stereotypically female attribute."[21]
- Mistake 42: Helping
- Mistake 46: Taking Responsibility
- Mistake 47: Following Instructions
- Mistake 65: Using Your First Name
- Mistake 69: Being Modest
- Mistake 81: Explaining
- Mistake 99: Tattoos and Piercings
- Mistake 100: Smiling Inappropriately
- Mistake 108: Sitting on Your Foot
- Mistake 111: Wearing Your Reading Glasses Around Your Neck

- Mistake 123: Putting Others' Needs Ahead of Your Own
- Mistake 132: Crying

To sum up *Nice Girls Still Don't Get the Corner Office*:

- Girl = loser, boy = winner
- Girl = boy = success
- Learn how to behave from society = wrong
- Learn how to behave from Lois Frankel = right

The more I read these kinds of books, the more I believe they're written by women who hate women. Why else would they mercilessly pick apart our behavior and beg us to change?

I'm also suspect of the incessant reminders that it's not our fault we're failures, and that if we listen to the author's step-by-step instructions and take her advice, she can lead us to the promised land (see the discussion of *Sex Today in Wedded Life* in chapter 2). It starts to sound like a cult. Is this about *helping* the sisterhood or *controlling* it?

I'm going to tell you another one of my pet theories, which I'm sure I'll get a lot of shit for. (But can it be any worse than listing *133* ways women suck?) I believe women like Frankel identify more closely with men and want power in the same way many men do. Because of that, I think these types of women look down on women, seeing their propensity for cooperation and connection as an embarrassment, the worst part of us. Eradicating female behaviors isn't an offensive idea to these women, because like many men, they view them as weaknesses.

There may be a shadow thread of hatred for women within books like Frankel's, and maybe even *Lean In*. I can't figure out why else they would consistently try to rid us of the very things that make us who we are. I don't identify with wanting to be the boss, but I don't give a shit if other women want to. More power to them! We don't *have* to be one way or the other. The only reason I can fathom that this angle dominates so much of feminism is because it comes from self-loathing and a desire to control.

The other pattern across these books is that none of them have worked. None have provided any workable or lasting solutions. Their suggestions, advice, and guidance haven't changed anything. The numbers haven't budged.

Perhaps it is because they're all trying to change women. And maybe, just maybe, it's because women aren't the ones who need changing.

WE DON'T LIKE SUCCESSFUL WOMEN

You need to be cold to be queen.

—BLAIR WALDORF, *GOSSIP GIRL*

In addition to not asking for things and being too nice, another explanation provided for the gender gap is the inverse correlation between success and likability for women. The more successful they become, the less others like them. The opposite is true of men, whose likability rises along with their success. This section examines the validity of this phenomenon, and more important, whether likability actually hurts women's chances of success in the corporate world.

Many research studies and lab experiments confirm that women are liked less when they become successful. One of the most well-known studies that's referred to throughout *Lean In* comes from Columbia Business School professor Frank Flynn and New York University professor Cameron Anderson, who divided students in half and asked each group to read the profile of a successful entrepreneur. The profiles given to the two groups were identical in every way, except for one important detail: in half of them, the person's name was Heidi Roizen, and in the other half, Howard Roizen. The students rated the entrepreneur on several dimensions, such as competence and respect, and how likely they would be to hire or work for the person. While many of the ratings were equal, the students found Howard to be a more appealing colleague.[22] This experiment and ones like it seem to provide compelling evidence that we do indeed find successful women less likable.

But if this were true, why is it that we love Oprah? And Ellen? And what about the adulation for Ruth Bader Ginsburg, whose status as a cultural icon recently inspired two separate movies that celebrate her life?

And is it only women who suffer a penalty for success? Ever heard the term "player hater"? As my hip-hop idol the Notorious B.I.G. says:

> We have the playas, and we have the playa haters
> Please don't hate me because I'm beautiful baby[23]

Anyone who's listened to a rap song knows that sometimes men face a negative reaction to their success. "Don't hate the player—hate the game" is the repeated refrain of such men, and similar experiences extend far beyond the realm of hip-hop.

How do we reconcile the conflict between what the research says and real-life examples that contradict it? That people dislike successful women but so many love Oprah? That women are the exclusive victims of this penalty but that Biggie suffers too?

The answer is this: *success* doesn't make a woman unlikable—a *desire for dominance* does. It betrays the expectation for women to be warm, communal, and cooperative. Sheryl Sandberg wasn't penalized as a child for being successful but for being bossy.

In general, people don't like being bossed around. But we like it even less when it comes from a woman. That doesn't make this attitude okay or justify ignorant behavior. It's wrong, and it sucks. However, we need to understand exactly what it is that sucks, so we can address it more effectively.

Now that we've specified what turns people off—not success in general, but more specifically, the desire to be in charge—how does that help us solve the problem? It appears to be an inescapable quandary for women who aspire to be the boss—traveling down the road to getting what they want makes them less likely to get it. Before we jump to solutions, the next issue we must tackle is whether being unlikable hurts their chances of ascending the corporate ladder. That is, how important is being liked to getting promoted? If it's a significant factor, then the catch-22 is worth our time and attention. If likability plays no role, or a minor one, then the penalty women suffer is unfortunate, but not one of the reasons they fail to get ahead. To answer this question, let's start off with a quick thought experiment.

Here's the set of *traits that fit a female stereotype*: cooperative, communal, warm, submissive, humble, unassuming, amenable, deferential.

And here are the *traits that violate the stereotype*: arrogant, aggressive, competitive, authoritarian, officious, domineering.

Who would you like better, a woman who exhibits the first set of behaviors or the second? For many people, their honest answer will only confirm the research at the beginning of this chapter.

But now for the more revealing question: Who would be more likely to get promoted to CEO of a big corporation—a woman who *fits* the stereotype, or the one who *violates* it?

It appears that fitting the stereotype of a woman would be a bigger challenge over the course of one's career. As a stereotypical woman, I can say from personal experience that being warm and unassuming never helped me get ahead. Quite the opposite. The bossy women always seemed to have the advantage.

I don't like bossy women. But I don't like bossy men either. I don't like people who try to assert authority over me while taking pleasure in the act. And this characterizes about 80 percent of the managers I've ever had, regardless of gender.

Through the lens of entertainment versus business, we can get even more clarity on the issue. Oprah and Beyoncé cannot be successful without adoration from their fans. In the entertainment world, being liked is your currency, and your success is predicated on it. How many people would've watched Oprah every day if they didn't like her? How many people would pay to see a film celebrating Ruth Bader Ginsburg if they had a severe distaste for her success?

Corporate America, on the other hand, is no popularity contest. People don't advance based on how much their subordinates like them. If anything, the opposite is true. Is it that we don't like women who become successful? Or is it that in order to rise to executive power in a big corporation, you have to be the kind of person who is feared and respected more than liked? Ruthlessness is almost a prerequisite for the job.

Is Hillary Clinton unlikable because she's a successful woman? Or is she just unlikable? For every Hillary Clinton there's also a Katie Couric. Lots of people dislike Donald Trump, but he won the presidency anyway.

Of course, not all female executives are unlikable. There were a handful of female executives in my career that I not only admired but also liked as people. The relationship between female success and likability isn't as clear-cut as we'd like to believe. Though I'm not convinced that being liked plays a large role in one's ability to break the glass ceiling, my individual experience and opinion aren't enough to validate this idea one way or the other. So, what does the research tell us? Does being disliked compromise career success? Does it decrease the likelihood of getting promoted?

LIKABILITY IN BUSINESS

Most scientific inquiries of this nature use what is commonly known as the "Big Five" paradigm. The Big Five are distinct categories of behavior that, when put together, encompass the entire universe of personality traits—*openness to experience* (intellectual curiosity, creativity, and a preference for novelty), *conscientiousness* (organization, dependability, self-discipline, and achievement orientation), *extraversion* (energy, assertiveness, and sociability), *agreeableness* (sympathy, kindness, and warmth), and *neuroticism* (degree to which one is prone to psychological stress).

Extraversion has several aspects that overlap with a male stereotype, and agreeableness loosely resembles the female stereotype. Extraversion describes behaviors along the dimensions of assertiveness and sociability. Those who score high on extraversion tend to seek stimulation in others' company, and they're often perceived as attention-seeking and/or domineering. Agreeableness manifests as a warm style of behavior—trusting, compassionate, compliant, and modest. People who are highly agreeable tend to be cooperative, and they're well-liked by others.

A study by Timothy A. Judge found that among the Big Five categories, the strongest predictor of who becomes a leader was extraversion, and the weakest was agreeableness.[24] It means that those who score high on extraversion are significantly more likely to rise to the top of the ladder than those who score high on agreeableness. The study's author noted, "Because agreeable individuals tend to be passive and compliant, it makes sense they would be less likely to emerge as leaders. However, once they reach the top, agreeable people may be more likely to succeed than those exhibiting the other personality types."[25] Another study by Truity Psychometrics supports this notion, finding that those who scored high on agreeableness were less likely to be recommended for advancement.[26] Their likability not only failed to get them ahead; it appears to be a liability!

The inverse correlation of likability and leadership also holds true for earnings; being well-liked doesn't pay. In their study "Do Nice Guys—and Gals—Really Finish Last? The Joint Effects of Sex and Agreeableness on Income," the Center for Advanced Human Resources examined several questions: Do agreeable workers earn less than disagreeable workers? Does the level of agreeableness impact wages differently for men than for women? If so, does it have a greater impact on male wages than female wages?[27]

The researchers indeed found that disagreeable men earned higher wages than agreeable men, and that agreeable men were punished twice: once for being agreeable, and a second time for having violated a male stereotype.[28] Because of this, agreeableness affected men's income more drastically than women's—men pay a higher price for being well-liked. Furthermore, the penalty for defying stereotypes was worse for men than for women overall. The wage gap between disagreeable men (conforms to type) and agreeable men (defies type) was much bigger than the wage gap between agreeable women (conforms) than disagreeable women (defies). The aforementioned study by Truity also demonstrates that the phenomenon applies not only to income, but to advancement overall. They found that agreeable men were recommended for advancement even *less* frequently than women with the same traits. In business, it appears that "beta" men are at a greater disadvantage than "alpha" women.

These studies and many others like them demonstrate that being well-liked isn't the key to career success. It appears to work the opposite way: disagreeable behavior—things that make you unlikable—confers the advantage. This isn't to say that women who want to be in charge don't suffer a penalty for it. They do become less likable when they act out of type. At the same time, it doesn't significantly affect their ability to break the glass ceiling. In fact, warm, likable women suffer far more than cold, bossy ones.

If you dig into it, the claim that women aren't more successful because they're penalized for success is really a frustration with stereotypes. Women who act against type are going to resent cultural norms for their behavior. As I mentioned in chapter 1, stereotypes can be damaging in many different ways. But stereotypes don't affect a woman's ability to succeed as much as we believe. Moreover, they appear to have a much larger impact on men than on women.

It's unfortunate that women suffer penalties for defying gender stereotypes. But this reality isn't the cause of the gender gap, and even if it were, what could we possibly do to solve the problem? We cannot control whether people like us or not. We can't legislate everyone's approval or demand that people accept our behavior. At some point, both men and women must accept that what we want in life won't always be appreciated by everyone. If you go after what you want, and people don't like you for it, the only option is to untether yourself from the need for their approval.

Conventional wisdom on the gender gap has focused almost exclusively on changing women so they acquire the traits and behaviors that will elevate them to the top of a corporate hierarchy. The first section of this book was meant to unravel these assumptions and demonstrate why they're untenable and undermine the very people they claim to help. As previously mentioned, the gender gap is a signal of a dysfunctional system, not dysfunctional women.

The remaining chapters explain why and how the system is to blame for the gender gap, and suggest a new way forward for both individuals and companies.

PART TWO

SEVEN

THE POWER REWARD

The lust for power is not rooted in strength but in weakness.

—Erich Fromm

Several years ago, at Google, we had to fill out a personality question-naire for a team off-site. When we arrived at the conference room at Google headquarters in Mountain View, California, Margaret from HR handed us thick, black booklets with the results. They were stun-ningly accurate self-portraits: details of our likes, dislikes, motivations, strengths, and weaknesses. Printed on the inside cover of each booklet was a color, which represented one of the four major personality types.

I was a Green. This meant I had a strong drive to help people, and my primary focus was on maintaining harmony. In other words, I was a hippie. To underscore the point, the color wasn't just called Green, but *Earth Green*. In the corporate world, this is akin to being a sex offender.

The polar opposite of Earth Green was Fiery Red. Reds are competitive and have a strong drive to be in control, and their primary focus is on results—as opposed to Greens, who prioritize relationships.

We were told to sit in groups with our like-colored teammates. As I sat in the corner of the room with my fellow Greens, Margaret reminded us, "No color or style is better than the other; each plays an essential role. This isn't a competition." The Reds booed.

My hand shot up to ask a question: "What are the colors of our executive leadership team?" Margaret shuffled her feet and hesitated before saying, "There are a few different ones . . . but . . . not all of them took the same survey. So, it's hard to say." Her nonanswer answer only fueled everyone's curiosity.

As the "middle children" in our personality rainbow, the Sunshine Yellows started getting antsy for attention and began chanting, "Tell us!" in unison until Margaret cracked like an egg.

Turns out, eleven out of twelve senior executives in the sales organization were Red. The Reds in the room went wild. Suck it, hippies! A Green next to me started crying.

Margaret cautioned us not to read a lot into it, but it was too late. We were stunned. It was laughable and made so much sense. I mean, what kind of hippie wants to be CEO? Red personality types want power, thrive in competition, and fear losing control. Isn't it obvious that they'd strive for roles in executive management and compete more fiercely to attain them?

Once you pass a certain salary, each subsequent raise makes less of an impact on your life and well-being. A $25,000 increase per year may be life changing when you make $75,000, but is hardly noticeable if you make $200,000. So, after you pass middle management in most organizations, power, in the form of management, is the exclusive reward.

Having power over others isn't universally motivating. If we think of it as a spectrum, people on one end derive immense satisfaction from this form of power, and they'll work harder and compete more fiercely to attain it. On the opposite end are people who not only find power unsatisfying, but also are uncomfortable in its possession. Instead, they derive pleasure and satisfaction from cooperation and strive for harmony in their relationships. Neither way is right or wrong; they're simply different threads in the human tapestry of motivation.

While the implications of this are quite obvious, it wasn't until our off-site exercise that it dawned on me for the first time: *of course people aren't going to work as hard for things they don't want!* Through the lens of color, my career trajectory (or lack thereof) snapped into full perspective. I didn't want to get promoted and manage people, because somewhere deep down, I knew those things weren't gratifying to me. For all my hard work, I wasn't getting anything I wanted in return. Until that day, I couldn't put those feelings into concepts and words that made sense. I had chalked it up to some mysterious personal failing and felt a sense of shame for what I thought was a lack of ambition.

Learning that my Fiery Red peers were motivated by power and control, I suddenly saw everything more clearly. I *was* ambitious, but I didn't want to work hard for a reward that was anathema to who I am. It freed up some of the guilt and shame too. There's nothing wrong with me! It's the system that's screwed up!

Rewards, of course, play a huge role in how hard people are willing to work to win a game. In most organizations, the near-exclusive form of reward is power over others. Research shows that men derive more satisfaction from positions of power and dominance, so they'll work harder to attain them, and it therefore shouldn't be surprising that they make up the majority of winners in the game. This isn't to say that women or Greens or whoever don't like or desire power. Professional authority isn't the definition of power. It is one *type*—one that's male-centric, and one that leaves many women unmotivated and unfulfilled.

What is power? It's a word that's used to represent so many different ideas, from physical strength to wealth and status. The historical narrative about power revolves around things like force, coercion, and control, and evokes images of presidents, high-ranking military and political figures, CEOs, and economic titans.

However, the past several decades of research and academic inquiry into the nature of power reveals a much different understanding of the term. The more comprehensive definition used by social and behavioral scientists is *the ability to produce a desired effect.*[1] While this includes physical ability to affect inanimate objects (e.g., a karate chop to a piece of wood), for our purposes, power is the ability to produce a desired effect in *others.* "Effect" can be an emotion (fear), an action (obey an order), or both.

Power is most often thought of in terms of one's status or position. For example, parents have power over their children, police have the power to lock you up, and managers have power over your livelihood. But this is only one type of power, and the more precise term for it, and how we'll refer to it going forward, is *authority.* Authority is granted or assumed and is based on one's position in a social structure or hierarchy.

Earlier, when I said that power is the near exclusive reward at work, I was specifically referring to authority. Managers can get a team to follow their orders because they've been granted formal authority to invoke negative consequences or withhold positive ones. People follow their boss's orders because the cost of disobedience is usually too high.

In contrast to authority, the other main type of power is *influence.*

While authority commands others' actions regardless of how they feel about it, influence requires their consent. It doesn't depend on a social structure or hierarchy, and it isn't granted by formal assignation. Rather, influence is cultivated through trust and exerted via relationships.

The simplest way to bring authority and influence to life is through the example of parents playing good cop/bad cop. Let's imagine a mother who spends most of her time nurturing her relationships with her children, connecting with them and building trust. When her kids act up, she isn't apt to enforce harsh consequences. Doing so would compromise their relationship, which makes her feel uncomfortable. Instead, she leans on the relationship as a form of power, appealing to their desire to please her and maybe even invoking a little guilt. ("I just made you your favorite dinner and do everything for you, and this is how you treat me?") When things get too out of control, or the behavior is egregious, she calls in the bad cop for reinforcements. ("Wait till your father gets home!") The bad cop doesn't come home and try to connect with the offending child by trying to build trust and understand why he or she misbehaved. The bad cop is all about consequences for having done so.

It's worth underscoring that one form isn't necessarily superior to the other; they're complementary forces, with each type serving a purpose in a specific context. While people use a combination of influence and authority throughout their lives, depending on context, most of us have a default, using one more than the other. We're comfortable when exerting the type of power that goes along our grain, and uncomfortable when flexing the type that goes against it.

For this reason, power is critical to understand when promoting diversity: With authority as the primary motivator in an organization, what does it mean for those who aren't motivated by it?

How does the preference for authority versus influence stack up across gender? A treasure trove of research confirms that men and women derive different levels of satisfaction from positions of authority at work. For example, a study in the *Journal of Health and Social Behavior* found that men who have the ability to hire and fire people are happier than men who don't, but that it's the exact opposite for women—those with the authority to hire and fire people were less happy than women without it.[2]

Whereas men are driven to achieve positions of authority and dominance, women are motivated to forge close relationships. Compared to men, they have a higher number of life goals, fewer of which focus on attaining power in a professional context. As such, they prioritize balance between their personal and professional lives instead of investing the majority of their energy in one direction. Ultimately, women view high-level positions as equally attainable as men do, but these positions are less desirable because they compromise women's broader life goals; the price for such advancement is too steep.[3]

In many ways, the idea that men and women experience power differently isn't new, nor is it surprising. It's not something most people have to spend years researching to understand. When people are surveyed on the differences between men and women at work, there's almost a universal agreement on the nature of those differences. In a CNBC article titled "Women in Power: Yes, They Are Different from Men," Jacqueline Corbelli, CEO of the advertising firm Brightline, says these distinctions couldn't be more obvious. "Women are good collaborators; we do it naturally."[4] In a *Fast Company* magazine article, "Women and Men, Work, and Power," several female executives are interviewed about their rise to the top and how their style differed from their male peers. Janice Gjertsen, director of new business development for Digital City New York, says, "I see the same patterns over and over again: Men are oriented toward power, toward making fast decisions in a black-or-white mode. Women are more skilled at relationships."[5]

It appears rather straightforward that corporations should expand the scope of rewards beyond authority if they want a more inclusive workplace. But this research isn't new, nor is the notion that men and women value different things. So, one must ask: Why haven't things changed?

———

The colors exercise helped me better understand myself, what motivates me, and it provided a new way to articulate what I wanted and needed at work. As I've mentioned, I'd long been held back by Google's requirement to manage a team. Before the off-site, I struggled to explain why my distaste for being a manager didn't reflect a lack of ambition. And I didn't know how to make the case for granting an exception to the policy. Armed with the insights from our exercise, I approached my manager with a renewed sense of enthusiasm. I figured that if I explained to her what I'd learned—that I'm motivated by building relationships and collaboration—she would understand that a managerial role would be more of a punishment than a reward, and somehow this would exempt me from the policy, and I'd finally get promoted. Perhaps more important, I hoped it would alter her perception of me. My hesitancy toward a management position would no longer be translated into "Marissa lacks ambition," and instead would be considered as, "Marissa knows who she is, and we need to give her rewards she actually wants."

Once again, my manager indulged my naivete with characteristic patience and politeness, and explained that the policy was what it was, and that it was unlikely to change anytime soon. She understood my point, but it was ultimately up to the VP of the sales organization, who despite having heard this argument before, remained steadfast in her view that managing teams was essential to one's career growth.

At first, I was dumbfounded. Why did our VP believe that everyone wanted the same things? Why wouldn't she want to motivate her best people to give their best effort? With time and experience, I learned what the academic textbooks and the studies could never teach me.

Our VP was a very smart lady. Of course she understood that not everyone wants to be a manager. But she wasn't about to change the policy to accommodate these people, because the policy was specifically designed to weed them out! What I saw as a simple difference in personality and motivation, she saw as weakness.

Convincing people that men and women relate to power differently isn't the problem—it's almost too obvious to deny. The real problem is that we regard men's relationship to power as strength and women's as weakness. And it's this value judgment, the association to weakness, that clouds so much of our dialogue on the topic.

For example, Harvard Business School released the findings of a study showing that women find professional power less desirable than men do. Although the study's authors were three highly accomplished, professional women, their research findings were mostly met with scorn. When Francesca Gino, one of the authors, presented the research at a conference, the audience booed her. As she describes it, "People were upset because they thought the paper suggested that we shouldn't offer women positions of power." She tried to clarify, but offering an explanation was never going to help Gino, because the people who booed her assumed that her findings implied that women are weak.[6]

Because men have dominated society, they've defined our understanding of power; their version is associated with strength and all else as weakness. But when you look at it from a nonmale worldview, you can see that men and women wield power in different but equally effective ways. If women don't want to climb to the top of the ladder as much as men do, it doesn't mean they're weak. Formal authority/control over other people isn't strength. Building relationships and seeking harmony isn't weakness. They're different ways of imposing one's will on the world.

COMPETITION VS. COOPERATION

Influence is inextricably linked to cooperation, as authority is to competition. Relationships can only thrive in cooperative environments, where winning doesn't come at someone else's expense. On the other hand, not every person can be the chief, so winning a position of authority is a competitive proposition by default. Those who are more motivated by the opportunity to exert influence also thrive in collaborative environments. While it may seem as though today's workplaces encourage employees to collaborate and tout teamwork as a company value, the truth is that more often than not, cooperative behavior is a barrier to advancement.

The stable of business literature over the past decade is filled with praise for cooperation's value and benefits. An endless stream of articles, from institutions such as *Harvard Business Review* and magazines such as *Fast Company*, herald teamwork as the foundation of today's economy and provide exhaustive guidance on how it's cultivated in the workplace. Instead of books dedicated to the virtues of cutthroat competition, our shelves are lined with ones like Adam Grant's *New York Times* bestseller *Give and Take: Why Helping Others Drives Our Success* (Viking, 2013).

It is curious that today's leading academic minds in business and organizational psychology believe that cooperation and other "helping" behaviors not only are possible, but also drive our workplace success. After all, a corporate hierarchy *is* a competition. Is it possible for cooperation and teamwork to thrive in a system that's a zero-sum game?

A study published in *Scientific Reports* shows that hierarchy is detrimental to human cooperation, regardless of whether individuals earned their rank, or it was assigned arbitrarily.[7] The findings support what most of us see so clearly from the trenches. People on a team may collaborate toward a common goal, but everyone knows that whoever does the best job at *claiming credit* for the team's work will end up as the winner.

———

Lois Frankel's number one female mistake is "Pretending It Isn't a Game." This mistake was brought to life with the softball game example discussed in chapter 6, in which a team came to the rescue of a physically injured opponent. In helping her, they sacrificed their chance at winning the game.[8] Frankel's point is that women prioritize others' needs and don't go for a win if it compromises their relationships, or others are hurt in the process. But business is a game, she reminds us, and you have to compete to win.

The notion that women need to embrace competition and forgo their inclination to cooperate is a popular one. Whereas Frankel seems offended that more women don't embrace competition, others are more practical about it. For example, in *Women Don't Ask*, authors Babcock and Laschever write that for the most part, women negotiate more collaboratively and that the female approach has plenty of advantages. However, they're also quick to remind us that our modern workplace is defined by competitive men, so acting collaboratively can be a disadvantage and reduces our chances of winning the game.[9]

Whether we acknowledge or don't acknowledge the value of collaboration, the lesson is the same. Since men set the terms and make the rules, we need to change ourselves to meet them where they are.

If winning power games at work were the best way for women to gain an advantage in society, I might support Frankel's and Babcock's advice. Life isn't fair, and if this is how the game must be played, then accepting it for what it is might indeed be the best way to go. But first we need to step back and ask: What is it we're trying to win, and who are we winning against? If competing with each other gets us a corner office, but we sit there sad and alone, can we call this success?

We've been so busy trying to erase the power differences between men and women that we've failed to recognize the power we already possess. We work in organizations that pit us against each other, eroding the fabric of friendships and undermining our most significant source of power in this world. For us to realize that power collectively, we first have to detach ourselves from the notion that climbing the ladder is the only way to achieve power in this world.

Instead of redefining women, we must redefine power and embrace the idea that one's position in a hierarchy means nothing about that person's ability to affect the world at large.

Today I sit at Starbucks, typing away on my laptop. I am a writer. I work alone, and my job is to get my thoughts on the page. I don't have employees or teammates, and there are no orders waiting to be filled. I don't earn a salary or receive a benefits package.

Am I powerless? Weak? Hardly.

At Facebook, it appeared that Kimberly enjoyed using her position of power to control elements of my career. After learning that I was fired, I hung up the phone and imagined Kimberly's face. The dead-behind-the-eyes stare and vacant smile. She'd finally won.

But did she?

It's been said that your enemies are your best teachers. I'd never thought of myself as a competitive person who needs to win. From Kimberly, I learned that's not entirely true. As it turns out, I *am* competitive, and I *do* need to win. But not the way Kimberly does it. Not at someone else's expense. No matter how things turn out with the book and my new career, I know that I've won. But that doesn't mean Kimberly lost. I was never competing with her in the first place. My triumph wasn't over Kimberly, but over myself.

Power doesn't have to roar. It need not coerce or control. Women aren't weak. Their power in this world might be less visible, but it's no less profound. Just as silk is stronger than steel, appearances can be deceiving.

EIGHT

IT'S THE SYSTEM, STUPID!

It is unbelievable how much you don't know about the
game you've been playing all your life.

—MICKEY MANTLE

Moneyball: The Art of Winning an Unfair Game, by Michael Lewis, is
a story about the Oakland A's in the early 2000s. In 2002, after losing
their three best offensive players to teams that had much larger budgets
than the A's owner allowed his team to work with, the new-look, low-
budget A's were written off as a lost cause.

Oakland's general manager, Billy Beane, was in a tough position.
Despite the insurmountable odds, Beane wanted to *win*. But how? The
typical strategies were unrealistic: scouting fresh talent (couldn't afford
it), raising funds (nobody would invest), or training the players harder
(didn't work). So Beane did what any other determined underdog
would do in the situation—he got creative.

At the time, talent was assessed and ranked by managers and

scouts who had decades of experience watching players in action and were experts in sorting out the good from the bad. Beane, however, decided to buck the conventional wisdom on calibrating talent, and instead turned to statistics. More specifically, a statistical analysis called sabermetrics, which crunched decades of data on performance and calibrated player talent on the basis of cold, hard numbers. While everyone considered the A's to be severely lacking in talent, sabermetrics told a different story.

Oakland's problem wasn't that its players lacked talent. It was that nobody, including baseball's most seasoned experts, could see the talent it already had. Sabermetrics ingested reams of performance data, more than any human brain possibly could absorb, so the program provided Beane with a much broader, more objective view of his players' strengths and weaknesses. He was able to see a trove of talent hidden within players everyone else had written off. Because of sabermetrics, Beane was able to leverage the full palette of talent on his team, and in doing so, he transformed the Oakland A's into one of the most successful franchises in Major League Baseball.[1]

One of the most poignant lessons from *Moneyball* is that we're really bad at judging talent in other people. But it isn't just a baseball thing; it's a *human* thing, which means we're also bad at knowing who's good at his or her job and who's not. This is a hard pill for most to swallow. We can all come up with a short list of people at the office who suck at their jobs; it all seems so straightforward. But look at what happened with the A's. Their talent was invisible even to the experts with decades of experience in baseball, to talent scouts whose entire job is knowing which players are good, and to their own manager, who should've known them better than anyone.

In Lewis's follow-up book, *The Undoing Project*, he explains why the A's were so severely underestimated: "Foot speed was overrated because it was so easy to see, for instance, and a hitter's ability to draw walks was undervalued in part because walks were so forgettable—they seemed to require the hitter mainly to do nothing at all. Fat or misshapen players were more likely to be undervalued; handsome, fit players were more likely to be overvalued."[2]

Scouts judged players based on what was most visible and most obvious, even though those criteria were poor indicators of talent. So why did the experts and scouts depend on them?

Our attention is a scarce resource, so we have to be selective about what we allow into our field of awareness. If our brains had to absorb every detail of reality and weigh them in some manner of logic and rationality, it would take so long we'd end up functionally paralyzed. Therefore, the brain relies on numerous mental shortcuts that enable quick decision-making and allow us to function in real time. But the speed and utility of these shortcuts also come at a cost. Since they disregard the vast majority of inputs in favor of a select few, they often lead us to make bad decisions and form erroneous conclusions. We're wrong about a lot of things, a lot of the time. The mental shortcuts we use to make decisions, and the resulting errors, are known as *cognitive bias*.

Sabermetrics, however, didn't suffer from these limitations. It didn't succumb to the same biases that plagued the baseball experts. Its objectivity allowed Beane to see which players were *actually* good, not just the ones who *looked* good.

The phenomenon isn't limited to the realm of sports. Our biases render us, as humans, incapable of seeing others objectively, and we're mostly unaware of these judgment errors. While the insight isn't necessarily new, we've yet to fully appreciate how much it affects who wins and loses in the game of business.

Consider that sports such as baseball already rely heavily on the observable. You either touched the plate, hit the home run, or you didn't. When there's disagreement, objective third parties (umpires) are relied on to make the final call. In sports, it should be easy to tell who's a good player and who isn't. But as we see in *Moneyball*, even when we watch the players with our own eyes and have data about their performance, we still can't discern good from bad.

The lessons from *Moneyball* hold even larger implications for the corporate world, where a win is far less straightforward, where we don't observe employees in action, and where we don't use objective third parties to solve conflicts and disagreements. In this chaos of ambiguity, our bias for visibility isn't only exacerbated—it practically runs the show.

The manufacturing economy of the early twentieth century was about making things. Companies at the time manufactured products such as steel, car parts, and petroleum, physical output that was tangible and concrete. If an employee is expected to assemble twenty widgets per hour, it's easy to determine whether he succeeded.

In today's information economy, the majority of corporate output isn't physical or concrete, and most employees aren't tasked with manufacturing a set of widgets during their clocked-in hours from nine to five. In place of physical production, we solve business problems, build strategies, create marketing campaigns, write code, manage teams, sell software, open accounts, build systems, and service customers. These are all things that are born not from a manufacturing plant, but from human intellect and imagination.

Output in a knowledge economy is mostly abstract and exceedingly difficult to measure, and people often disagree on what success looks like. Multiply this lack of clarity across thousands of people doing thousands of different jobs, all with intangible, ambiguous long-term outcomes. It becomes incredibly difficult to draw clear lines between the work people do and its business impact. High performance is hard to detect, and low performance is easy to cover up. It's virtually impossible to discern any person's impact; a strategy could appear awful in the short term but turn out to be transformational in the long term. If the person responsible is evaluated before the results had time to unfold, at best she'll get no credit for her brilliant contribution, and at worst she'll be blamed for its supposed failure. In today's workplaces, it's hard to tell who's doing good work, or even who's doing work at all.

The swirl of corporate ambiguity is blinding, and in the absence of clarity, what we *can* see becomes the ultimate arbiter of talent, competence, and performance. The people who *talk* about their work, *promote* their work, and spin their work to *sound* impressive are perceived as doing a good job and as having leadership qualities. What's important isn't whether your strategy was a brilliant success or a spectacular failure, but how you *looked* in the process.

In his article "Why Our Brains Fall for False Expertise and How to Stop It," Khalil Smith wrote, "People often pay closest attention to the person who talks most frequently . . . and when our brains are left to their own devices, attention is drawn to shortcuts, such as turning focus to the loudest or tallest person in the room."[3] Smith points to research showing that even when members of a group agree on which one of them is the subject-matter expert and best suited to make a decision, they defer to him or her only 62 percent of the time. The other 38 percent? They listen to the most extroverted person in the room. Why? Because extroversion manifests in behavior such as excessive talking and dominating conversations. Extroversion is practically defined by its visibility. Another experiment referenced in the article found that people estimate someone's influence based on the amount of time he or she spends talking. "Airtime" turned out to affect perceptions of influence more than credibility and expertise did.

It's not just visible behaviors, like talking, that fool us. Studies show that physical features, such as height, are correlated with dominance, positions of leadership, and larger bonuses at work.[4] Height, in particular, is positively correlated with earnings and authority level in both the workplace and the military; the average height of those in managerial positions is higher than those in subordinate roles.[5] In his book *Blink: The Power of Thinking Without Thinking*, Malcolm Gladwell points to the statistical anomaly that 14.5 percent of men in the United States are six feet or taller, but of *Fortune* 500 CEOs, that figure is 58 percent. He argues that being short is likely to be as much a hindrance to success in corporate America as being a woman is.[6] And it's not only height that confers an advantage. Even seemingly minor and random things, like the width of one's face, affect our perception of competence. A *Leadership Quarterly* study found that men with wider faces negotiated a $2,200 higher bonus than their more narrow-faced brethren.[7]

Nassim Nicholas Taleb captures the sentiment in his book *The Black Swan: The Impact of the Highly Improbable*:

> We love the tangible, the confirmation, the palpable, the real, the visible, the concrete, the known, the seen, the vivid, the visual, the social, the embedded, the emotionally laden, the salient, the stereotypical, the moving, the theatrical, the romanced, the cosmetic, the official, the scholarly-sounding verbiage (b******t), the pompous Gaussian economist, the mathematicized crap, the pomp, the Académie Française, Harvard Business School, the Nobel Prize, dark business suits with white shirts and Ferragamo ties, the moving discourse, and the lurid.[8]

Visible traits and behaviors used as proxies for leadership and competence include, but aren't limited to, aggression, self-aggrandizement, loudness, bluster, overconfidence, and height. Subtler things, such as empathy, listening, humility, introspection, quietness, and being short don't draw our attention, and people disregard them accordingly. In environments characterized by blindness and ambiguity, they're almost invisible. What can be seen becomes more important than what's real.

A critical point in all of this must be underscored: the first set of traits isn't inherently superior or more valuable than the second. And those traits aren't more highly correlated with competence or leadership ability. They are, however, more highly correlated with men.[9]

One type of cognitive bias is called *overconfidence*, and it refers to people's tendency to be overly certain they're right. The godfathers of cognitive bias, Daniel Kahneman and Amos Tversky, have written extensively on the subject, explaining that overconfidence leads people to be too sure of their predictions, as well as the source of their mistakes. According to Kahneman, overconfidence is the most damaging of all the various mental biases. In fact, when asked which one of our hardwired shortcuts he would choose if he had a magic wand and could eliminate one, his answer was overconfidence. It has been blamed for a range of global calamities, such as the sinking of the *Titanic*, the *Exxon Valdez* oil spill, the nuclear disaster at Chernobyl, and even both world wars.[10]

Moneyball isn't the only book Lewis wrote describing the large-scale consequences of cognitive bias. In *Boomerang: Travels in the New Third World* and *The Big Short: Inside the Doomsday Machine*, he dissects various financial disasters, from Iceland's economic collapse to the 2008 subprime mortgage crisis, and tells us that at their core, they are stories of male overconfidence. He says male overconfidence is a theme that runs through every book he's written that addresses large-scale financial calamity. In an interview with *Forbes*, he noted, "I'm amazed that women put up with it. I'm just amazed that after the financial crisis they didn't come in and say, 'No more men running financial institutions.'"[11]

For their landmark research paper called "Boys Will Be Boys," two economists analyzed the performance of three million stock transactions over a six-year period. While men believe they're better stock traders than women and think they're smarter about stocks than other people, the evidence told a different story. Not only did it show women as the winners in trading stocks, but a single-woman household did better than a household with a man and a woman, which did better than households with only a single man. It appears that the more men involved, the worse things went.

Men in the study didn't fare worse because they weren't as good at picking stocks. The problem was that they were too certain they were right about a particular stock, so they traded nearly 50 percent more often than women. The flurry of trades drove up their costs and lowered their returns.

In a phone interview with the *New York Times*, one of the study's authors, Brad M. Barber, said, "In general, overconfident investors are going to be interpreting what's going on around them and feeling they are able [to] make decisions that they're really not equipped to make." He suggested that more men respond to short-term financial news, trying to make sense out of what amounts to nothing more than meaningless "noise."[12]

Another study, by the investment company Vanguard, found that during the 2008 financial crisis, men sold more shares when the market bottomed out, likely taking big losses as they missed the rally that followed. John Ameriks, head of Vanguard Investment Counseling and Research and a coauthor of the study, suggested that male investors, as a group, appear to be overconfident. "There's been a lot of academic research suggesting that men think they know what they're doing, even when they really don't know what they're doing," he said. On the other hand, when women aren't sure of something, such as the correct evaluation of a stock or direction of the market, they appear more likely to acknowledge it and refrain from acting on incomplete information.[13]

Unwarranted certitude often results in lots of activity and quick decisions. When you know you're right, there's no need to take the time for careful deliberation or to weigh the cost versus the benefit. Considering potential risks is unnecessary, because when you're certain of something, there's no perceived risk. So, you act. You make big decisions. And you do it frequently.

One reason overconfidence fuels success at work is because the activity it engenders is usually mistaken for progress. The researchers who wrote "Boys Will Be Boys" observed people's trading habits and data over a six-year period before declaring which gender fared best. And the numbers at the end were indisputable.

In the work world, people are evaluated regularly, without a number to capture their return on investment (ROI). Imagine how the study might have turned out if the researchers had to determine the better traders while subjected to the same constraints we are in the corporate world. No doubt, the men's *volume* of activity would be a proxy for progress. The frequent trading would likely be seen as evidence that the men were working harder, putting in more effort, and making forward movement. Their certainty, although often unwarranted, would be mistaken for confidence and considered leadership material. On the other hand, the women's lack of activity would likely be seen as weak and overly cautious, and perhaps considered evidence that they were less motivated and not as good at their jobs.

At work, we don't have the benefit of long-term hindsight to judge who was right, who was wrong, and who *really* deserved the better grades. When people don't know or agree on what it means to do a good job, doing *something* becomes the barometer for success. It doesn't matter how useless the something may be—what matters is how many somethings you did and how bold they appeared. In such environments, overconfidence is almost a prerequisite for success.

———

There are two general approaches to problem-solving, both of which, at their core, are about changing people's behavior. The first strategy involves trying to change people directly: convince them why they should change, then provide direction about how to do so. The second approach is systemic or environmental. Changing certain elements of a system or environment can alter behaviors without any direct appeal to the individuals within it.

By employing various training and leadership programs, most corporations have tried promoting more women into power using the first strategy. All over the country, company workshops have sprung up to teach employees how to overcome unconscious biases, and female leadership programs abound, where women learn how to be more assertive and ambitious. These training and thought-leadership efforts continue to fail time and again, because as any social scientist will tell you, the worst way to change people's behavior is by teaching them how to change their behavior.

In one of his most well-known TED talks, behavioral economist Dan Ariely tells us that the most effective way to alter people's behavior is by making changes, even small ones, to the system or environment in which they're operating. Such situational tweaks are more effective than appealing to people directly, even when it's in their best interests to change. For example, people understand that exercise and healthy eating will help them lead a longer, healthier life. But this knowledge alone, no matter how often it's repeated, has done little to reduce the nationwide obesity epidemic.

Ariely brings the concept of systemic/environmental change to life with an intriguing example about organ donation. He shares a chart of organ donation rates across the European Union. The rates vary drastically between countries. For example, in Denmark, 4.5 out of 100 people give consent for organ donation, while in Austria that number is 99.98 out of 100.[14]

During my women's leadership presentations at Google, I'd share Ariely's chart with the audience and ask everyone to imagine that they're the head of a committee tasked with increasing the number of organ donors across the European Union. With only six months to solve the problem and a budget of $1 million, I'd ask people to share some approaches they might take. The most common suggestions were along the lines of education, increasing the information available (pamphlets, videos, etc.), incentive programs, advertising campaigns, marketing, outreach, and so forth. There was also a general consensus that most solutions would exceed a $1 million budget and take longer than six months, but that's always expected with large projects that have seemingly unrealistic constraints.

Then, I'd tell everyone that the hypothetical situation wasn't exactly imaginary. Years ago, the European Union formed a committee to increase the number of organ donors, and they were given six months and a $1 million budget to complete the project. It took them only seven days to set their plan in motion and only three months before the rate of organ donors jumped an astounding 80 percent. Oh, and the budget? They only used *$10,000* (1 percent of the $1 million allotted).

How did they manage such a Herculean feat? The answer is shockingly mundane: they changed the form at the DMV. When the committee looked at the countries with the fewest organ donors, they found that their DMV forms asked people to check a box if they wanted to become an organ donor. People weren't checking the box, so they weren't becoming organ donors. European countries with high donation rates had a slightly different form, which said something along the lines of, "Check the box if you *don't* want to be an organ donor" (emphasis mine). People weren't checking the box, so they were becoming organ donors.

In their book *Switch: How to Change Things When Change Is Hard*, Chip Heath and Dan Heath capture the sentiment of people versus environment: "What looks like a people problem is often a situation problem."[15] They open the book with a story about a research study designed to see whether the size of a popcorn container affected how much popcorn people would consume. The unwitting subjects of the study were moviegoers who received either a medium or a large bucket of free popcorn as they entered the theater (they weren't allowed to choose the size). The experiment had a twist: the popcorn they were given was so wretched one person compared it to Styrofoam, while others asked for their money back. The question at the heart of the study was whether the size of a person's bucket affected how much nasty popcorn he or she would eat. And the answer was a resounding yes. People with larger buckets didn't eat just a few more pieces, but 53 percent more than those with smaller ones. This might have made sense if it were regular movie theater popcorn, but when something tastes like Styrofoam packing peanuts, the only sensible explanation is that the bucket size affected how much people ate.[16]

In 2014, the Food and Drug Administration began requiring chain restaurants and movie theaters across the country to display calorie counts on their menus. The new requirements were an effort by public health experts to combat the country's obesity epidemic. They believed that if Americans saw how many calories were in their favorite foods, they'd think twice before ordering, and they hoped that the new regulations would have substantial impact. At the time, the nationwide obesity rate for adults was 37.7 percent. In 2018, the rate was 39.6 percent.[17] People don't change their behavior simply because it's the best thing for them or the right thing to do. Giving them more information about their bad choices doesn't help. It's an approach to societal problem-solving that has proven ineffective time and again, and the gender gap is no different.

Only 4.8 percent of *Fortune* 500 companies are run by women.[18] We've tried to increase that number by trying to change everyone in corporate America, but mostly by trying to change women. We've told them to lean in, go for the promotion, be more assertive, more ambitious, more confident, and less fearful. We've tried training people to overcome their cognitive biases and prejudices. We've tried to get organizations on board by showing them that diversity improves their bottom line.

We've been trying to change people's behavior the same way we've tried to solve nationwide obesity: by explaining why people should lose weight and how to do it. And with similar results. That is, none at all.

The reason systemic change is so critical for a problem like the gender gap is because it's the only way to overcome cognitive bias and the mental limitations that cause us to choose more men in the first place. In chapter 9 we'll explore more detailed systemic adjustments that help overcome bias, but for now, the point is that we must change our perspective on the problem. We must shift away from seeing women as both the source of blame and the key to resolution.

The examples above might seem overly simplistic. Change a form from opt in to opt out. Reduce the size of containers. How could there possibly be a simple change in design to solve one of the most stubbornly persistent societal issues of our generation? Maybe there isn't.

What do I know? I'm not a behavioral scientist. But I do have a few ideas!

How about . . . oh, I don't know . . . offering more than *one* type of reward for a job well done? Like, the stuff women actually want? Instead of discarding their stated desires as a relic of oppression, what if we *listened* to the kinds of things they need, want, and deserve? Like more flexibility, acknowledgment, and universal childcare or subsidized preschool? What about being able to trade in some part of your salary for the ability to work from home three days a week? Or offering at least *one* type of win that doesn't require your peer to lose? How about establishing measurable goals that the whole team is responsible for achieving, instead of individual goals that come at others' expense?

These might not appear as simple as tinkering with a DMV form, but they're exactly the kinds of design adjustments that impact behavior. And we've barely tried any of them. Instead of tweaking the system to better fit the diversity of people, we've been trying to tweak people to better fit the conformity required by the system.

If design solutions appear so simple, why haven't we tried them? One reason is our ignorance about behavioral change. Not everyone has read the latest research on the most effective means for large-scale change. So, we continue down the known path of educating and training people directly, believing that if we keep pushing, one day we'll get there. But I also think there's another, perhaps deeper, reason for the lack of pursuit of such changes.

Systemic improvements require corporate executives and CEOs to change their companies in ways that, if effective, would result in them losing power. And most people like that enjoy their power a little too much to let a thing like gender diversity get in the way. It's easy for a CEO to publicly declare his dedication to the cause when he doesn't have anyone holding him accountable, and the methods he employs have never worked in the first place. CEOs like this get all the applause without being on the hook for doing anything meaningful. One might even argue that leaving the problem unsolved *benefits* the people at the top, since there's no threat to the power structure, and their positions are more secure.

Furthermore, the systems that require change are the same ones that put these people in power in the first place. Many senior men and women seem to have the attitude that because they figured out how to win the game, things must be working just fine. To them, it's *everyone else* who's the problem.

This is why I believe the first, most critical step is recognizing that the system is biased toward selecting male traits. Whether powerful people will take the steps necessary to fix the system is a different story. But at least we can all be more honest about what's at play instead of sinking time and energy into solutions born from powerful people's rhetoric and agendas. Bringing the truth to light also helps prevent phony declarations from corporate executives who wave the banner of feminism publicly without taking action to fix things in their own backyard.

———

Billy Beane didn't go from underdog to champion by trying to change his players' behavior. He didn't try to increase their ambition, encourage their self-esteem, or use top players as role models they should emulate. He did it by employing a system—a system that better assessed player talent and didn't rely on mental bias and proxies such as foot speed.

When it comes to solving the gender gap, we've tried to change behavior directly instead of changing broken aspects of the system. It's akin to trying to convince every person at the DMV to become an organ donor instead of simply redesigning the form.

PART THREE

NINE

A NEW WAY FORWARD

*Leadership almost always involves thinking and acting
like the underdog. That's because leaders work to change
things, and the people who are winning rarely do.*

—SETH GODIN, *TRIBES: WE NEED YOU TO LEAD US*

One day over lunch at Facebook, John, my colleague on the marketing team, told me a story about his plan to finally exceed expectations
and get his much-deserved promotion. At the time, our job was to
create pitches and marketing material for the Facebook sales teams
to use with clients. Since the salespeople were the ones using what we
created (we didn't sell to clients directly), it was too difficult to measure the impact of our work using standard metrics, such as revenue.
The best way to know whether we were doing a good job was to ask
the sales teams. And when it came to John, their feedback was glow-
ing. They declared him a star, saying the work he did was more than
just valuable—it was the secret sauce behind their record-breaking

year of sales. For a role like ours, you couldn't do much better than that; the sales teams held up John as the example for all of marketing to follow.

Despite his exemplary work, John kept receiving "meets expectations" on his performance reviews. For a while he was confused by the average scores, and then one day he discovered what he was doing wrong. During lunch, he confided in me about the insight that was putting him on the fast track to a promotion.

"I realized I wasn't doing enough publicity for myself with the marketing team. I was too focused on my job for sales. So, I started emailing the marketing managers more often and now post several times a day in our Facebook group."

"And what do you say in the emails and posts?" I asked incredulously.

"It doesn't even matter," he explained. "I'll copy article links from the trades, post a pic from an event, anything really. And my manager has already told me how impressed the marketing team managers are with my recent improvements in performance."

"But our performance is based on what the salespeople say, not what marketing people think."

"That's what I thought too."

Oh.

John was right. And that's why he was successful. He had figured out the rules of the game we were playing. Even though our job was helping salespeople, and they were the only ones who could judge the merits of our work, the marketing managers had ultimate say over how our performance was evaluated. As soon as John started focusing on making them feel important instead of on his actual job, he improved his scores.

————

When I first read the bestselling book *The 48 Laws of Power* by Robert Greene, I was nothing short of appalled. With laws such as law 2, "Never put too much trust in friends, learn how to use enemies"; law 3, "Conceal your intentions"; and law 15, "Crush your enemy totally," Greene codified selfishness and dishonesty as the central means of gaining and abusing power.[1] By the time I got to law 21, "Play a sucker to catch a sucker—seem dumber than your mark," I was convinced the whole thing was a joke. I mean, what kind of person adopts law 17—"Keep others in suspended terror: cultivate an air of unpredictability"—as a success strategy? And then it dawned on me: the type of person who succeeds in corporate America.

Over the years I'd read a ton of books and research on business, management, and leadership, and they all had a wildly different take on the rules for success than Greene. *The 48 Laws of Power* stood in direct contrast with everything I'd known to be true. As I read it, I wondered which school of thought was more credible. And much to my dismay, after finishing Greene's tome on power, I realized that when it comes to the corporate world, he was right.

The wisdom dominating modern literature on business and management is based on the assumption that employees are rational and everyone works in the interest of the business. That people who perform best get promoted. That your position in the hierarchy is a meaningful signal of your competence and leadership skills. That there's a linear relationship between your work and your results, or your impact and your success. None of that is true or real, because a corporation isn't a microcosm of the real world. It's mostly a game for power, where winning is about political savvy, not necessarily competence, leadership skills, or talent.

The 48 Laws of Power gave me a new lens on the world I'd been living in for the previous fifteen years. I could see how these laws had been played against me time and again. Had I known what game I was playing and had I understood the rules, I would have fared much better. I'm not saying I would have climbed higher on the ladder. I wouldn't have necessarily adopted the tactics to get ahead—it's not in my nature—but I could have made better decisions and protected myself against unnecessary loss. I would have seen things for what they were and lowered my expectations about what my career could provide; namely, that it would never bring me the kind of fulfillment, recognition, and autonomy I sought.

If we imagine different contexts as different games, like school vs. work vs. sports vs. art, it's easy to see that each one has distinct rules for winning. Greene's laws don't translate to academic success, nor would they work if your goal were to be a songwriter. I can't imagine Martin Luther King Jr. or Mother Teresa having the same impact on society if they'd used Greene's laws as a guide to their behavior. Their strengths don't manifest in a game where law 12, "Use selective honesty and generosity to disarm your victim," is a rule for winning. On the flip side, I can't imagine President Trump succeeding as a social justice warrior or even as the coach of a basketball team. Different games, different rules, different strengths required. And in the corporate game, *The 48 Laws of Power* is the closest I've ever seen to an honest playbook. The winners of the corporate world have personality traits that lend themselves well to law 2, "Never put too much trust in friends, learn how to use enemies." That's why you don't see many tortured-artist types wind up as CEO.

The first step in achieving meaningful diversity is being honest about why the workforce isn't diverse in the first place. As mentioned in chapter 8, that means we have to get honest about the game we're playing and the rules by which it's governed. People are diverse by their nature. The reason it's not reflected at the top of the corporate world is because only so many people can obey laws such as law 14, "Pose as friend, work as spy." It's not diverse because only a small subset of human behavior is recognized and rewarded. Diversity doesn't happen by trying to mold everyone into the same narrow template. It doesn't happen by forcing people to adopt one set of rules and a singular definition of success. It happens in exactly the opposite way: by letting people be themselves. It happens by holding up truth and objectivity as the values that govern our organizations, so we can better see the full scope of diverse talent sitting right before our eyes.

This chapter explores ways that companies can change the rules of the game—first and foremost, by creating the conditions that foster trust and honesty, so people can be themselves and contribute their full range of capabilities. It involves a larger variety of rewards, rethinking leadership roles, and building the necessary systems to identify talent and impact more objectively, moving us away from our use of male behaviors as proxies for competence. As you read the chapter, you might note that it's the first and only one in the book that doesn't focus on women. But women aren't the cause of the gender gap, which means they aren't specific to the solution, so they need not be addressed directly. True diversity is about variations in how people think, their perspectives, talents, and experiences. *That* is what we should be solving for, and if we do it right, a more balanced ratio of men and women is the inevitable result.

TRUTH AND TRUST

One of the most poignant themes in Greene's book is a hostility toward truth. The theme is also reflected throughout the corporate world, where most workplaces are characterized by a distinct lack of honesty and candor—zero-sum games, managing up, political language, jargon, and the unspoken rules around who's allowed to say what.

Systemic dishonesty breeds distrust, and such distrust is at the center of almost all flavors of corporate dysfunction. It not only leads to a lack of diversity but also crushes creativity, reduces productivity, and makes companies unable to adapt to change.

To understand the correlation between trust and business outcomes, consider Google's research on the topic. Over the course of two years, the search giant quietly conducted a study to isolate the factors that made teams effective and successful. They went into the study believing the answer would lie in the right mix of talent and skill but came out with a totally different conclusion. The researchers found that success wasn't determined by the skills, experience, and talent of the team members, but *how* the team worked together.

More specifically, there were five key ingredients for effectiveness.[2]

1. **Psychological safety:** Do we feel safe to take risks on this team without feeling insecure or embarrassed?
2. **Dependability:** Can we count on each other to do high-quality work on time?
3. **Structure and clarity:** Are we clear on everyone's goals, roles, and expectations?
4. **Meaning of work:** Is our work personally important?
5. **Impact of work:** Do we fundamentally believe that our work makes an impact?

While all factors were important, only the first was a fundamental requirement. Without psychological safety as a team's backdrop, success was impossible. In the same way a person has to meet her basic needs for survival (air, water, food) before she can achieve things such as self-esteem, a team has to meet the need for psychological safety before it can achieve anything of value.

Psychological safety is another way of saying trust. In an environment of trust, people can express their ideas without fear of judgment or ridicule. When people trust each other, they're more willing to take risks because they're not afraid of making mistakes or failing. Perhaps more important, trust is the condition required for people to feel comfortable being themselves.

Google includes the following in their report: "Individuals on teams with higher psychological safety are less likely to leave Google, they're more likely to harness the power of diverse ideas from their teammates, they bring in more revenue, and they're rated as effective twice as often by executives."[3] When people can be themselves and don't feel their success is predicated on fitting a mold, the pool of ideas, perspectives, and leaders will be as diverse as the individuals on any given team. In that sense, creating conditions that value truth and cultivate trust are the natural antidotes to myopia and homogeneity. Workplace diversity doesn't happen by force; it's not achieved through quotas or trying to change people. It's the exact opposite: it is the natural result of an environment in which people can be themselves.

BUILDING A CULTURE AND SYSTEM OF TRUST

Organizing around the values of truth and trust doesn't mean increasing the trustworthiness of each individual employee. It's about building reliable systems that people can trust to be fair and objective, not arbitrary and punitive. It means a system that's not exclusively zero sum and that doesn't force one person to lose when another one gains. These systemic changes create win-win conditions for each party, improving employee well-being *and* the bottom line.

One company that has triumphed in its pursuit of objectivity and trust is Bridgewater Associates, the largest hedge fund in the world. Started in CEO Ray Dalio's two-bedroom apartment in 1975, Bridgewater now has the highest cumulative net profit of any hedge fund that ever existed.[4]

Early in his career, Dalio understood the limits of the human mind relative to knowing which ideas are any good and which people have any talent. He also understood that to overcome such limitations, he'd need tools to help him see things he ordinarily couldn't. As Billy Beane used statistics, and orchestras use a screen for auditions, Dalio uses algorithms. Algorithms are at the core of Bridgewater's tools, allowing them to make decisions based on objective measures instead of proxies and guesswork.

One such tool is called the Dot Collector, which Dalio described in detail during his 2017 TED talk.[5] He explains that the Dot Collector tracks employees' ideas and decisions over time, allowing the company to judge each person's contributions more objectively and in ways they wouldn't ordinarily be able to do. As such, the Dot Collector can determine how people think, which ones are more believable, and which ones should have a bigger say in decision-making—all merit-based inputs instead of rank and status.[6]

While technology underpins Bridgewater's ability to remain objective, it's just one part of the overall system, and alone, it isn't enough. The foundational element of objectivity is in Dalio's words, "radical truthfulness and radical transparency."[7] For the tools to work effectively, people need to say what they believe, be who they are, and see that truth in others. In the same TED talk, Dalio shares an anecdote about a man who works for him named Jim Haskel. After attending a meeting run by Dalio, Haskel shot him an email saying he deserved a D– for it, that Dalio had come off as disorganized and unprepared. Reflecting on the incident, Dalio says, "Isn't that great?" The great part wasn't that he got a bad grade for his performance, but that Haskel had the freedom to share his perspective, even if it was unflattering, even when it was about his own boss. Radical truthfulness and transparency require that people be honest, regardless of where they sit in a power structure. The technology lets Bridgewater employees speak honestly, because they trust the *system* will decide what constitutes talent and good work, not the emotions of their superiors or other arbitrary factors.

BALANCE OF POWER

In the closing chapter of his book *Principles*, Dalio warns readers that none of the tools he has discussed will help an organization if it doesn't have proper governance, which he describes as an "oversight system that removes the people and processes if they aren't working well."[8] An oversight system provides checks and balances of power, to ensure that the interests or agendas of one particular person or group is never placed before the needs of the community and business as a whole.

It makes sense that Dalio believes so strongly in checks and balances. Without them, power gets concentrated at the top, truth and transparency cannot survive, and people no longer trust the system. A power structure without checks and balances results in tyranny, whether it involves citizens of a country or employees in an organization. And tyranny cannot coexist with truth.

The concept of checks and balances is a simple and universal principle of organizational health, and it applies in a wide range of contexts, not just corporations. Perhaps the best way to understand the implications of this concept is to use a simple example. Let's take a neighborhood pool, the kind owned by country clubs or small, seasonal businesses. It's well accepted that the lifeguards have the power and authority to make decisions based on what's best for the swimmers. If there's lightning on the horizon, the lifeguards make the call to close the pool regardless of whether revenue will suffer. If these decisions were solely up to the pool owner, safety would be compromised. But the lifeguards hold a degree of power, allowing them to enforce rules that protect users' safety over the business's interests. It is that simple a concept—power should be bestowed upon a variety of decision makers who represent a variety of interests that span beyond profit.

Despite the progressive ethos of Silicon Valley tech, CEOs have near-absolute power, and not a single company has instituted even the simplest, most basic checks and balances of power. One might argue that this isn't entirely true, since CEOs are accountable to a board of directors or shareholders (if the company is publicly traded). Still, CEOs control all communication to these constituents and can easily design messaging to serve their own interests. Furthermore, a board of directors, and even shareholders, are all guided by the interest of the bottom line, not by the interests of the people working at a company. The CEO's power *within* the organization and *over* its workers is near-absolute. That means reality is subjectively decided by those with the most power, and employees must accept it or risk their livelihoods. It's tyranny by another name.

Absolute power at the top of a large organization—and the distrust it engenders—wreaks havoc on profit the same way absolute power of a pool owner would wreak havoc on the safety of its swimmers. It just does so in ways that are less visible and less immediate than a drowning. While we want to believe a CEO always has profit at the top of his or her agenda, this would be a foolish assumption, as human nature is based on self-interest, and checks and balances are a way to neutralize the effects of one person acting too much on such instincts. Furthermore, we can't expect corporate executives to always make the best or smartest decisions, even when they're acting in the interest of the business.

One example of a business disaster wrought by a CEO's unilateral action is detailed in Chip Heath and Dan Heath's book *Decisive*. In 1994, the Quaker Corporation paid a staggering $1.8 billion to acquire the beverage brand Snapple. At the time, the CEO of Quaker, William Smithburg, was driven to make a big splash in the market, seeking the kind of validation and success he'd garnered the decade before when he made the decision to purchase Gatorade. Although the Snapple acquisition would leave Quaker in debt, Smithburg saw it as a way to quell his fears of a hostile takeover. The Snapple purchase was less about profit and more about ego. The debt it would incur was bad for Quaker but good for Smithburg; he saw it as job security. Today, the Snapple decision is considered among the most disastrous decisions in the history of business. In an admirable show of humility, Smithburg reflected on the situation by saying, "We should have had a couple of people arguing the 'no' side of the evaluation."[9]

Capturing the poignant lesson of the story, the Heath brothers wrote, "Under Smithburg's leadership, Quaker was contemplating the largest acquisition in its history, with deal terms that had been mocked widely by industry analysts, and yet, unbelievably, there was *no one within Quaker arguing against the acquisition!*"[10]

Is this story all that surprising though? When a CEO wants something, and his or her personal interests or ego are invested in the decision, it's unwise of his or her subordinates to argue against it. This is the kind of business disaster that can be averted by a distribution of power. When acting against the interest of someone with total power over your livelihood, how often are the best decisions going to be made? Distributing authority across various stakeholders can only improve the quality of business decisions over time, as long as there's a process in place to ensure it doesn't compromise speed and efficiency.

A common argument against checks and balances is that corporations shouldn't be structured like the government. As private entities, they're designed to maximize profit, not to protect the people they employ. But I'm not saying we should model organizations after the government, only that we should adopt a specific principle: that power left unchecked is bad for people and bad for business.

The founders of Google must have understood this, because they instituted a fairly unique power structure in the company's early days. Not to protect employees from abuses of power, but to protect confidentiality and the security of information.

Years ago, at Google, I had a manager named Sean, a well-liked and well-respected rising star in the organization. It wasn't only Sean's superiors who adored him but our whole team. Twice we banded together and nominated him for Google's most prestigious, if unoriginally named, "Great Manager Award." With a sterling reputation, a loyal team, and a great work ethic, it seemed as though Sean were poised for a lifelong, lucrative career at the company.

Arriving at the office one Tuesday morning, I passed Sean in the hallway, and he seemed more hurried than usual. As I walked into the conference room for our weekly team meeting, it became immediately clear that something big was up. Leslie, the SVP of our business organization, was seated at the head of the conference room table. She made a somber gesture toward the chairs, and we sat down. With a flat tone, she broke the news: Sean was no longer with the company. She wasn't able to say much more about the circumstances, and nobody spoke. There were no questions, only stunned silence.

Sean called each of us over the next few days and explained what had happened. Google had acquired lots of small companies in the five years since he'd started, one of them a boutique technology firm called AdStart. He had worked closely with the AdStart team over the years, and it was run by a close friend of his, Nancy. Nancy had left Google several years earlier, but the majority of the people she'd managed at AdStart remained.

Google had recently decided to shut down AdStart and redeploy people across new roles at the company. When Sean found out, he contacted Nancy and suggested she email the team to express her support. Taking his advice, Nancy sent each person a note with well wishes for the impending transition and their new journey at Google.

The problem was that the news about AdStart wasn't public information. Only senior directors like Sean were told about it, in an email that was explicitly marked confidential.

None of the salespeople on the AdStart team knew it was being shut down and they were going to be redeployed, so as you can imagine, Nancy's note came as quite a shock. Several people on the team went straight to management, demanding to know what the hell was going on. When Michael, the head of Google's security team, investigated the source of the apparent leak, he quickly found the confidential email that Sean had forwarded to Nancy.

Sean's intentions were commendable; he was trying to garner support for a team that was going to need it. As he explained it to us on the phone, it was a foolish thing to do, but his heart was in the right place. Given these circumstances, it's reasonable to assume Sean would've been given the benefit of the doubt, especially in light of his status in the company as a hardworking leader who was universally respected and admired. But the story goes that, as soon as Michael discovered the confidentiality breach, his decision on the matter was instantaneous. Sean had to be let go.

At first, our executive team didn't see Michael's decision as final. Sean was considered a great friend by many of the most powerful people in the organization, and they were confident they could flex their position and have Sean let off the hook with a warning.

But here's the fascinating part: it didn't matter what the executives wanted because, as it was explained to us, Michael had absolute power to make the decision that was in Google's best interests. He remained uninfluenced by the pleas of Google's most powerful people, even when the conflict reached all the way to the top of the company. Not even the most powerful executive at the company held sway over Michael's decision.

One of Google's core values is sharing information with employees up and down the ranks. They would famously report earnings, financial growth numbers, and other highly confidential information every week, with the entire company. And with that kind of privilege comes great responsibility. Googlers are expected to take confidentiality seriously, and Michael was the one responsible for making sure they did. As I recall a senior leader once explaining, in Google's early days, Larry Page and Sergey Brin took an ingenious step in making sure security and confidentiality would be upheld as core values of the company. They separated that division from the power matrix, so they weren't influenced by politics. Google gave Michael full authority to make decisions in the interest of company security, not in the interest of power.

It appeared that Michael felt the situation with Sean was much more clear-cut than our sales leaders did. Sean had shared confidential information outside the company. On top of that, he was a senior director, which meant he had even more responsibility to uphold Google's culture. Michael's position was that *not* firing him for such an obvious violation would send the wrong message to employees. It would mean the rules didn't apply to everyone equally, and the sacred tenet of confidentiality could be overridden if you have the right friends in the right places. So, in the end, it was Michael's call, and that call was to have Sean fired.

Security is so critical to Google's bottom line, they gave the team its own power of authority. The rules were black-and-white, and Michael had the power to enforce them. It always struck me as odd that given the amount of time and money Google invests in hiring the best and brightest minds, there was no version of Michael in human resources. In contrast to the security team, HR had almost no power; for the most part, they were ruled by the executives they served. Is security of information more important than the security of the people who were expected to uphold it?

Google isn't alone here. Few, if any, large corporations imbue HR with the power to make decisions in the best interests of their employees. The function is almost always there to serve those in power and protect the best interests of the business.

With all of the recent conversations about #MeToo and abuse of power, the simplest of solutions rarely seems to appear. Checks and balances on power are the only way to ensure that people are protected from abuse, and that means abuse of any kind, not just sexual harassment. If people like Michael were at the heads of every HR department, it might not become a utopian world, free of abuse, but it would go a long way in restoring a modicum of trust among employees in an organization.

MOTIVATION AND REWARDS

Rewards play one of the most significant—and perhaps least discussed—roles in diversity. If everyone were motivated by the same things, life would be one long battle over a handful of resources. The fact that we are unique in our desires is precisely what enables a free-market society. If I love rice and you love fruit, we expand the circle of available resources, which creates the opportunity for trade. Collaboration in this regard is considered the force that propelled human civilization. As Harry Browne, author of *How I Found Freedom in an Unfree World*, puts it, "Diversity is the source of harmony in human relationships."[11]

As discussed in prior chapters, the only reward for ascending the corporate ladder is power and control over others, which means that from the beginning, the scales are tipped in favor of the subset who is motivated by it. A diverse set of winners depends on a diverse set of rewards. But what does winning look like if it's not a supervisory role? Perhaps an even better question is: What do people want?

Studies over the last few decades are conclusive about what motivates great work and what people want from their employers. The most valuable reward, the one that inspires the greatest work, is recognition. It ranks higher than pay increases, promotions, or training.[12] Recognition for good work almost seems too obvious, which makes it all the more surprising that, according to research by *Forbes*, 83 percent of the organizations they studied suffer from a recognition deficit. Unsurprisingly, they found that the top 20 percent with a "recognition-rich culture" had 31 percent lower voluntary turnover.[13]

Promotions and pay raises are usually considered equivalent to recognition, or at least a form of it, but they are *incentives*, which isn't the same thing. Recognition is a broader concept that means acknowledging and showing appreciation for a person's or team's contribution, effort, and/or outcome. Social scientist and *New York Times* bestselling author Dan Ariely reports the conclusions of a study showing that "when we are acknowledged for our work, we are willing to work harder for less pay, and when we are not acknowledged, we lose much of our motivation."[14]

Confusing incentives with recognition blinds us to the bigger picture of employee motivation and what people need to do their best work. The Gallup organization suggests that small gestures of appreciation, such as a personal note or thank-you card, are just as effective and meaningful as large incentives, as long as they're honest, authentic, and tailored to the needs of each individual.[15]

Motivation also changes based on whether rewards are achieved via competition or collaboration. As I elaborated on in chapter 7, some people are motivated by competing in win-lose scenarios, while others are more moved by collaborating toward win-win outcomes. It bears repeating that neither preference is superior to the other. They're inherently neutral and reflect natural differences across the spectrum of human personality. These differences become problematic only when people who prefer to collaborate are forced to compete, or those who prefer to compete are forced to collaborate. In both scenarios, motivation and performance suffer in a significant portion of the group. Competition isn't right and collaboration isn't wrong, so it only makes sense to adopt both systems, letting people work in ways that best suit them. They'll be happier and more productive and will do better work, making it a win-win for both a company and its employees.

WELL-BEING, BAD BOSSES

Perhaps the biggest threat to trust *and* profit are bad managers. According to a *Forbes* article, "Regardless of one's level in an organization, your day-to-day relationship with your direct manager is invariably crucial to your well-being."[16] If employees feel, among other things, that their supervisor takes a real interest in their development, or offers frequent praise and recognition, they're likely to be engaged.

No matter how many perks or how fancy one's office space, they hardly compensate for a tyrannical micromanager lording over you and your work every day. It's impossible to improve organizational trust without rethinking the scope of a manager's authority and how companies deal with bad bosses.

Management is a universal prize given without consideration to whether a person is capable of the task. Given the steep price a company pays for a bad boss, it's astounding how little attention is paid to the matter. Being a great manager, or even just a moderately good one, requires a specific skill set. Just as you wouldn't hire an accountant to lead the creative department, placing people without management skills in the role of a manager is almost always a disaster. The problem is often addressed with management training. But for the most part, turning a bad boss into a decent one requires years of learning, practice, and a deep commitment to change. Or a lobotomy.

Google has made an honest attempt to address the issue of bad managers over the years. One mechanism they use is called the "Upward Feedback Survey," or UFS.[17] The UFS is a chance for employees to rate their managers on a range of criteria, such as their level of support, feedback, and consideration, and how likely they are to recommend their manager to others. The survey is anonymous, so people are fairly honest and eager to fill it out. Managers are also required to share the results with everyone on the team, and the public shame of a bad score is believed to be a significant motivator in improving managers' behavior.

The Upward Feedback Survey is certainly an enlightened approach to encouraging good management, and it gives employees a modicum of power in what's otherwise a one-sided relationship. However, in my time at Google, the UFS had one fatal flaw: a manager's score, no matter how bad, didn't matter.

My friend Daryl was once under the thumb of a power-mongering, narcissistic manager named Barry. Barry's UFS scores were abysmal. Daryl's team took a sort of perverse pride in the fact that Barry scored as the worst manager in our whole organization. Since Google didn't share scores between teams and you couldn't compare managers directly, Barry's team did a field study. They told everyone they knew what Barry scored and never found anyone whose manager fared worse.

You can imagine everyone's surprise when the next month, Barry was promoted, which meant that he'd soon be managing twice as many people. Apparently, his UFS feedback didn't impact his performance scores or affect his candidacy for a promotion. I mean, why should *competence at being a manager* be a factor in someone's performance as a *manager*?

Google also encouraged lateral moves, which meant people moved roles every few years. Like any other applicant, you had to go through a series of interviews with the hiring manager and others on the team. The hiring manager also had access to the history of performance scores for internal candidates, a useful data point when considering whether or not to hire someone. Internal candidates, however, weren't allowed to see the UFS scores for the hiring manager, which would also serve as an incredibly useful data point in deciding whether you wanted to work for them. I always found that strange. Why can't employees see if you're a bad manager, but managers can see if you're a bad employee? Managers practically make or break an employee's happiness and performance at work, and Google went to great lengths to emphasize the importance of having good managers. But when it came down to it, the measures were meaningless. They didn't protect good employees from unwittingly choosing a poor manager, nor did they prevent bad bosses from widening their circle of negative impact.

Good intentions at the top and survey tools are helpful in many ways, but they aren't enough to prevent bad managers from affecting well-being or reducing employee morale. The fact remains: a hierarchy grants bosses near-absolute power over their subordinates, and employees have little to no recourse when suffering under a bad manager. In most cases, the only option to neutralize toxic or abusive supervisors is reporting them to human resources. But most people understand the unwritten rule about HR: the department is there to protect the company, not the employees. When there are no meaningful ways for employees to neutralize the power of a bad boss, trust in the system is destroyed.

TRUST AND PRODUCTIVITY

The corporate hierarchy is a construct that was created for the manufacturing age, a time when workers were as interchangeable as the parts they handled—cogs in an industrial machine, who had no choice but to listen and obey. On an assembly line, for instance, there was no such thing as taking a break when you felt like it or putting in a fraction of effort when you weren't in the mood to go full out. The choice to stop working, even for a moment, had an obvious effect on output, and consequences were immediate. Because companies held all the power in the relationship, workers had little to no recourse. This system may have been effective when employees were making *things*, but when they're applying *intellect*, the system becomes massively dysfunctional.

In knowledge work, the majority of a company's supply comes in the form of brainpower, stored in the minds of a workforce that has the choice of whether or not to apply it. Output isn't immediately visible or concrete, making it easy to pretend you're working hard even while doing nothing at all. What companies fail to appreciate is that when people reduce their effort, this leads to a direct reduction in supply.

That is, productivity and efficiency depend on how hard employees are *willing* to work, which is mostly governed by how well their employer treats them.

Who hasn't had a moment at the office where you decide there's just no more work that's going to get done that day? Such decisions can be caused by a run-in with a controlling micromanager, a hangover, or the realization that the only thing you seem to be getting in return for all your hard work is relentless frustration. In these moments, the instinctive reaction is to put in less effort or throw in the towel altogether. Add up all the people with this attitude in an organization on any given day, and you have a *major* supply issue. It's not only day-to-day engagement that impacts supply but also retention.

In the early twentieth century, employees who left their job on an assembly line didn't take the company's resources along with them. Their vacancy was filled with another warm body to perform the same mechanical tasks. When knowledge is the currency, however, employees who leave their job take a precious piece of supply along with them and often leave their teams scrambling to fill the gap.

These aren't thought exercises and what-if scenarios. According to the Gallup organization, only 13 percent of employees at work are engaged. The rest are classified as either "not engaged" or "actively disengaged,"[18] which is another way of saying 87 percent of employees aren't doing any work. This abysmal supply level is analogous to Henry Ford waking up one morning and deciding to set fire to 87 percent of his factories.

Human capital is *expensive*, and it makes business sense to ensure that investment is well spent. Just as Henry Ford was obsessed with productivity, every CEO today should be obsessed with making sure his or her employees are engaged during the workday. And yet, it's often among the lowest priorities on a C-level agenda. How important is a company's long-term strategic plan if only 13 percent of your work-force is going to act on it?

The key to increasing efficiency in a knowledge economy comes down to creating systems employees can trust to protect their interests and meet their needs. Supply rises and falls based on how people are treated, so their well-being is a crucial factor in a company's overall success.

Some people believe that companies can't possibly be, nor should be, responsible for making employees happy. They argue that effort and hard work are prerequisites for happiness, and employees aren't happy in their jobs precisely *because* they're disengaged and not making the necessary effort. As such, employee engagement is presented as a chicken-or-egg situation that can't be solved or legislated by a corporate entity.

This concern is invalid for a couple of reasons. The first is that optimizing toward well-being doesn't mean a company is responsible for making sure every person in a company scores high on the happy scale. The way corporate systems are set up today makes it almost impossible for employees to feel respected and trusted enough to be fully engaged with their work. Changing those conditions isn't just the moral thing to do, although it can be argued as such. It's the best strategy to maximize productivity and avoid putting the metaphorical torch to 87 percent of their supply. Modern psychology and behavioral economics have proved the link between certain environmental elements that lead to well-being and translate into increased effort and productivity. To dismiss them as being outside the realm of responsibility means a business must accept the dysfunction that results. Those who want to make the best decisions in the interest of their bottom line and/or their employees can't afford to ignore what we know to be true about worker productivity.

CREATIVITY AND INNOVATION

Today's economy is characterized by relentless change, which means creativity and innovation have never been more important. They are forces that make it possible for people and organizations to adapt. However, most corporations crush creativity and stifle innovation for one of the same reasons they lack diversity: the system destroys trust.

Creativity is often misunderstood, and it can be defined various ways. For our purposes, let's consider creativity the ability to look at things in novel ways and to combine different ideas to form new ones. Innovation is the implementation of a creative idea to improve something or make something new. The current stable of business literature hails the virtues of such forces, and there's an endless stream of thought-leadership books, articles, and videos dedicated to these topics. Innovation in particular is painted as some mysterious and inexplicable force that only pops up in sacred places, like Pixar and Google. Companies spend millions of dollars trying to capture just an ounce of the innovation streaming out of Silicon Valley tech.

But the innovation process is simpler and more straightforward and boring than its mythic status implies. It's nothing more than test-launch-iterate. Or guess-experiment-retry. Innovation happens by applying the scientific method to business stuff. That's. It.

However, if it's that easy, why is it so hard? Why—after all the articles in *Harvard Business Review*, all the books written in its name, and all the management consultants hired to make it happen—can't people grasp such a simple thing? Why is it so hard for companies to innovate if it boils down to a process we learned in sixth grade?

In his book *"Surely You're Joking, Mr. Feynman!"*, physicist Richard Feynman, winner of the Nobel Prize and one of the most lauded minds of the twentieth century, describes two incidents early in his career that taught him why innovation can be so difficult. The stories weren't related to his work on the Manhattan Project, or Feynman diagrams (illustrations capturing the behavior of subatomic particles), or his pioneering work in the field of quantum computing. They happened when Feynman was a teenager and spent the summer working at a hotel his aunt owned.

In the first story, Feynman was working in the kitchen, cutting string beans in the manner his boss prescribed. But he soon discovered a much more efficient way of handling the beans and was able to cut significantly more of them in a shorter time. Feynman was excited to show off the idea to his boss, but during the demo he lost focus and pressed his own finger into the knife. As blood squirted from his finger onto the beans, the boss yelled, "Look at how many beans you spoiled! What a stupid way to do things!" Feynman notes that it was a careless, preventable mistake, and that his idea was still a good one. But, as he laments, "there was no chance for improvement."[19]

The second story involved Feynman's work answering phones as a desk clerk at the same hotel. At the time, phones had switches and wires, which meant he was tethered to the desk during his shift. He came up with what he thought was a brilliant idea: tying papers and threads to the switch, he could answer the calls from some distance away, freeing him up to do tasks he otherwise couldn't while tethered to the desk. When his aunt (also his boss) arrived on the scene, she got angry with him for making things more complicated and creating a mess to boot. He tried to explain that he'd made it *easier* to answer calls, but as he says, "You can't say that to anybody who's *smart*, who *runs a hotel*!" Feynman concludes the chapter with what he learned working in the kitchen and at the front desk of the hotel that summer: "Innovation is a very difficult thing in the real world."[20]

The innovation process is the same, whether you're cutting vegetables or coding software. While the *process* is simple, the *mind-set* it requires is hard. This mind-set is brilliantly captured in Feynman's stories. Neither of his innovations was perfect—he cut his finger and made a bit of a mess with the phones. They both needed a couple more iterations before they were great. But he never got the chance to tinker with them because the people in charge couldn't tolerate mistakes and preferred clinging to how things had always been done.

Innovation and experimentation involve a series of incremental moves. Your role in the process is to observe whatever outcome appears and use it to figure out where to go next. The most valuable outcomes are mistakes and failures, because they shine a light on what's wrong. You can think of failure as the cane showing a blind person where to walk; if it hits a wall, he knows not to go there. So, in that sense, failure and mistakes are the light pointing you in the right direction. In Feynman's case, cutting his finger was a mistake that gave him the idea of wearing thumb guards. But the boss saw the mistake as evidence the entire idea was stupid. And that's why innovation is so difficult, as he lamented. Those with power over you, whether in a corporation or a kitchen, might not have the same relationship with uncertainty and failure. It's only human to see these as threatening, and only human to try to mitigate the uncertainty that can lead to failure in the first place. But innovation cannot survive in these kinds of environments. It needs a safe space for people to try and fail without threats to their livelihood and sense of self.

Because innovation depends on responding to failure, it's a well-known ethos of progressive tech companies. At Facebook, one of the posters that hangs on the wall of almost every conference room says, "Fail Harder." But this was an empty platitude, because most people aren't wired that way, and the system still rewarded certainty and penalized failure. No number of posters could change that. There was also a lack of understanding about what "fail harder" means. When someone did a bad job on a project, people would excuse their shoddy work by waving the banner of "We 🖤 failure," which is a total perversion of the message.

As a tenet in business, failure doesn't mean that nobody is accountable for mistakes, or that when something fails we simply hold our heads high (although we should). Failure isn't the goal. It's not something to strive for, or something that should be celebrated for its own sake. Failure is valuable only as a precursor to learning. For example, at Google, engineering failures required something called a "postmortem" document, which provided details on what failed and why.

For a few minutes in August 2013, Google went dark. During that time, no one in the world was able to access Google search, Gmail, YouTube, or any other Google property. In that handful of minutes, internet traffic dipped by 40 percent[21] and based on revenue estimates at the time, cost Google over half a million dollars in advertising revenue. In the company's view, it was a colossal and inexcusable technical failure. You can imagine that at most companies, the fallout of such an event would be toxic and politically fraught, as employees scrambled to cover their asses and escape blame. At Google, it was the exact opposite. Instead of pointing fingers, the engineers responsible for the fiasco posted a detailed analysis of what went wrong and why, and it was available internally for anyone at the company to read.

That is an example of how to institutionalize failure in a company culture. By emphasizing the learning, growth, and innovation it engenders, not the failure itself.

TRUTH AND TRAGEDY

On January 27, 1986, the night before the space shuttle *Challenger* was set to take flight, in the privacy of his home, NASA engineer Bob

Ebeling told his wife that the *Challenger* was going to explode in the morning, and everyone on board would certainly die.

The next day, on January 28, from the floor of my first-grade classroom, I watched Ebeling's private prediction become a public nightmare, as the *Challenger* was torn apart over the Atlantic Ocean, only seventy-three seconds after takeoff. I was too young to understand what was happening, but in that moment, the shuttle exploded, killing all seven astronauts on board, including the first teacher in space, Christa McAuliffe.

To investigate the cause of the tragedy, President Reagan formed the Rogers Commission, and following their investigation, the term "O-rings" entered the national lexicon. The O-rings were the infamous rubber insulation gaskets that malfunctioned, breaking the seal of the rocket boosters, and ultimately leading to the fatal explosion. Even now, more than thirty years later, if you ask anyone over the age of thirty-five, "What caused the *Challenger* explosion?" more often than not, they'll refer to the O-rings, even though most of us aren't sure what they are.

Another thing most people don't know is that technically, the O-rings didn't malfunction; they worked exactly as intended. The engineers who created them knew they posed a danger in colder temperatures, and when the weather forecast made it clear that on January 28 the temperatures would be in the low twenties, they rang a loud and clear alarm. Calling a meeting the day before launch, they warned management that the O-rings might fail in temperatures below sixty degrees and urged for a delay. Engineer Brian Russell also sent a frantic memo to NASA managers two days before launch. Titling it "HELP" to capture their attention, he begged them to hold off, citing risks associated with the O-rings in lower temperatures. Despite the warnings, NASA's management team chose to move forward and launch the shuttle on schedule.

With these facts in mind, it's hard to say the O-rings are to blame for the *Challenger* explosion. Imagine a car that's designed to operate safely at speeds below 120 miles per hour. If a driver knowingly violates the safety standards, taking the car for a joyride at 180 miles per hour, spins out, and crashes into a tree, do we blame the accident on the car, or on the careless, negligent driver?

In addition to O-rings, the Rogers Commission reported another, perhaps more significant, source of blame for the tragedy. The same thing investigators would also blame seventeen years later, when the spaceship *Columbia* disintegrated upon its return through the Earth's atmosphere, killing all seven astronauts. In both cases, the stage for disaster was set, not by technical failure but by NASA's organizational culture. In particular, the report described its culture at the time as highly flawed, and one that downplayed risk and silenced dissent. As the report states, "We are convinced that the management practices overseeing the space shuttle program were as much a cause of the accident as the foam that struck the left wing."[22]

NASA is an organization of our best and brightest scientists and engineers. How is it possible they were foiled by something like culture, *twice*, when human lives were at stake? Language is a funny thing. An ambiguous, ill-defined term like "organizational culture" makes it easy to dismiss. Culture is largely considered an afterthought, or as a luxury for Silicon Valley companies with lots of venture capital and extra cash in the bank. "Company culture" conjures images of employees playing foosball while eating free snacks and holding team off-sites in Hawaii. It feels soft. Secondary. A nice-to-have versus a must-have. But when we say it was organizational culture that caused two national tragedies and fourteen deaths at NASA, it doesn't mean a lack of Ping-Pong tables and free-beer Fridays. It describes an organization's attitude toward truth.

When referring to the source of failure at NASA, the Rogers Commission reported that the space agency lacks "effective checks and balances, does not have an independent safety program and has not demonstrated the characteristics of a learning organization." They go on to underscore the importance and urgency of fixing the communication systems, saying, "The board strongly believes that if these persistent, systemic flaws are not resolved, the scene is set for another accident."[23]

When power is too concentrated, among an individual or a group, truth is almost always the first casualty. People instinctively understand they must go along with reality as legislated by those in power, and that dissent in any form, whether warranted or not, is threatening. NASA, like most corporations today, had no way of neutralizing power, of separating agenda from truth. This might seem like a dramatic parallel to make, but it's no less accurate. Consequences aren't usually as disastrous or as public as a space shuttle explosion, but they're no less real, and they leave a dramatic impact rippling in their wake.

CONCLUSION

Diversity happens when companies and organizations create conditions of trust so that people feel comfortable being themselves, offer a variety of rewards, allow both competition *and* collaboration, design systems to better evaluate performance, and rebalance power in the employee-employer relationship (e.g., by providing meaningful recourse for bad management). The gender gap cannot be solved by trying to make everyone the same. It is solved by allowing everyone to be exactly who they are.

Structure, like our organizational systems, drives behavior, not the other way around. Demanding new behaviors inside old systems is always a losing proposition. The opportunity lies between what we want our organizations to be and the current reality. But a new way forward must go deeper than leaning into our ambition, potential, and promotability. It goes beyond new policies and proactive measures to close the pay gap, secure the pipeline of women coming into the organization, reduce the parenthood penalty, increase boardroom diversity, or eliminate unconscious bias. A new way forward requires a revolution in organizational thinking and management models oriented toward truth and objectivity, capturing our collective brainpower and capacity to create better products, services, and yes—a better world.

To create that new reality, we must face existing truths about women, power, and the workplace. Then, we must change the rules of the game.

TEN

WELL-BEING VS. WINNING

When a measure becomes a target, it ceases to be a good measure.

—MARILYN STRATHERN

In 2014, President Obama declared, "The average full-time working woman earns just 77 cents for every dollar a man earns . . . in 2014, that's an embarrassment. It is wrong."[1] The wage disparity between men and women has been coined the "wage gap" or "gender pay gap," and in 2017, it reached 80.5 percent.[2] Solving this problem has been a priority in the public discourse on gender equality. As Hillary Clinton, Sheryl Sandberg, and Betty Friedan all have noted, equality will only be achieved when money and power are evenly distributed between men and women. As such, the success of modern feminism—and by extension, the progress of women in America—is measured on just two dimensions: money and power.

There's a saying, "You get what you measure," and it means that people work toward the metrics they're held against; what we count becomes what we do. If a company wants to keep expenses down, one way they might do this is by measuring how much each salesperson spends on entertaining clients. Knowing their expenses will be tracked more closely, salespeople will likely be more prudent in their restaurant choices or entertain clients less often.

While measurement provides a useful feedback mechanism that helps us stay the course so we can achieve our goals, we often forget that the behavior we're measuring isn't the goal itself. We don't track employee spending simply to keep costs down, but to keep profits up. If salespeople reduced expenses by a record amount, but this action compromised profit because deals were lost and revenue suffered, would we declare it a win?

When we get too focused on the "how" (cutting expenses, etc.) and lose sight of the "why" (profit), we can move ourselves further away from our ultimate goals. That's why we must be thoughtful and deliberate in choosing what we measure, and consistently examine whether it's moving us in the right direction.

As a measure of gender equality, power and money are not just meaningless—they've also compromised the larger goals of feminism and work against the best interests of women overall.

THE GENDER PAY GAP

There's a widespread misunderstanding about the gender pay gap in America. When President Obama declared that women earn "77 cents for every dollar a man earns," it sounded as if he was saying that women are paid less than men for the same jobs. But the reason female wages are lower is that we choose professions that are less lucrative.

For example, women dominate teaching and nursing professions, while men dominate the finance and banking world. Once you adjust for the differences in hours worked, job experience, level, and choice of profession (e.g., teacher versus investment banker), the wage gap shrinks from 80 to 96 percent.[3] In other words, it's not that Company X pays their male managers more than they pay their female managers; rather, it's that Company X has fewer female managers overall. Using the adjusted 96 percent figure, different wages for the same job can, at most, explain only the remaining 4 percent.

Since the gap in earnings is primarily due to women's career choices, the only way to close it is for women to choose different jobs or to climb the ladder at higher and faster rates. To that end, dozens of nationwide campaigns have sprung up encouraging women to choose fields such as finance and STEM, which have higher average salaries than female-dominated industries like teaching and nursing. Efforts to place more women in executive roles also falls into the category of solutions for the wage gap, since senior roles have higher salaries.

If women suddenly broke the glass ceiling en masse, occupying half of all executive roles and half of all STEM professions, the wage gap would disappear. But the question we need to consider is: As what cost? Asked another way: If we successfully close the gap, would women be better off?

DOLLARS AND SENSE

Money is a tool for achieving the larger goal of well-being, not the goal in and of itself. My friend Jenna once joked that she'd give Google $75,000 of her salary back if they'd agree to fire her sociopathic manager and let her team have a say in his replacement. Jenna's boss was a nightmare, and she felt powerless. Regaining a shred of human dignity from nine to five was worth half of her yearly income. Could anyone blame her?

There are miserable CEOs and unhappy rich people. Money is useful only to the extent that it helps us live out our desires and is spent in accordance with what we value as individuals. One woman may prefer more flexibility over a higher salary, while another may value material luxury over a part-time schedule. Comparing these two women, and by extension, comparing anyone, on the basis of income is meaningless; it tells you nothing about which one is more successful.

I'm not saying that women don't like money. I'm not saying that it's okay for men to earn more than women for the same exact job. My point is that comparing the total earnings of men and women, without consideration for the trade-offs it entails, isn't just a meaningless indication of progress—it potentially threatens the interests of the very people it's intended to serve by compromising what's arguably far more important: their well-being.

As we saw in chapter 2, only 18 percent of women desire to be a top executive. The reasons they gave were things such as the lack of balance, the amount of politics, and disinterest in the job. But female progress is measured in money and power, so success requires women to discard these reasonable concerns in favor of metrics set by other people. Are we to believe that a higher income will compensate for the downsides that taking a job they don't want entails?

If working longer hours or managing more people or playing more office politics reduces the quality of our lives in the long run, how can we call this a win? Because men have more than we do? More *what*? At some point, we have to ask ourselves: What exactly are we winning, and who are we winning against?

The key point is this: solving the pay gap by measuring progress in dollars, can require many women to act against their own well-being, and that's the *opposite* of empowerment and progress.

One must also wonder what men are being measured against. If we're striving for an equal world, where women run half our companies and men run half our homes, why aren't we measuring the time men are investing in household chores and child-rearing? There are no national campaigns funded by the White House encouraging men to work more flexible jobs, or to come home earlier so they can get dinner ready and help the kids with their homework.

Women earning more money isn't the only way to close the wage gap. It can also be closed by men choosing more flexible jobs, so they can pitch in more at home. Or if they stayed home altogether to raise their children and run the household. And if they did go that route, it would give women more of the balance they desperately crave. But few, if any, people ever look at it from that angle, asking, "What do women need and want, and how do we measure progress against it?" Instead, people declare, "Men are in the ideal position in society, so we'll measure ourselves against them."

The wage gap argument is also built on a limited understanding of how money confers power onto the people who possess it. A million-dollar stash sitting in a box under a mattress is, in and of itself, meaningless. It's just a box full of paper. The power of money is realized only when it's spent. This might seem like quibbling over semantics, but it's a critical distinction. Money gives power to the person *spending* it, not the one *earning* it.

Even when women aren't the ones earning the majority of money in a household, they're often the ones spending it. Dhanusha Sivajee, EVP of editorial and marketing at XO Group Inc., says that women are the most powerful consumers in the economy: "Whether women are working or even if they are at home, we see that women drive 70 to 80 percent of all consumer purchases [globally]. . . . Even if women are not making the transaction they are still impacting the decisions because they are the primary caregiver of children and the elderly."[4] In the United States, women control more than 60 percent of all personal wealth and account for 85 percent of all consumer purchases.[5] In light of this expanded view, the assumption that women will have more power when they earn more money is false.

Measuring the wage gap as we do today tells us nothing meaningful, and closing it wouldn't necessarily translate into a world where women are better off (at least in societies like the United States). Which raises the question: When it comes to equality and its service to the best interests of women, what *should* we be measuring?

WINNING VS. WELL-BEING

If you get what you measure, we should be measuring ourselves against the single most important metric: well-being. Isn't that the best way to capture our ultimate pursuit in life? To create a meaningful and fulfilled existence? By "well-being" I don't necessarily mean happiness. I mean it in a broader sense. The feeling that your life is under your control. That we're choosing our goals consciously, and that those goals reflect our authentic desires and harness our strengths.

Focusing on well-being both helps us lead better lives individually and better serves the needs of women at large. With well-being as the goal, we can direct effort and resources toward the social problems that are *truly* the biggest barriers for female progress. For example, only 18 percent of women report having the desire to be a CEO, but what if 80 percent of women wish they had more access to affordable childcare? If we're trying to serve the best interests of all women, and not just the interests of a handful of women, which desire would we focus on? A well-being metric directs our focus in ways that serve the greater good and helps stave off personal agendas that can co-opt those efforts. It democratizes feminism by empowering women to do what they want to do instead of telling them what they *should* want to do. It restores the original "free to be you and me" spirit of feminism, which has been perverted into "free to be what *I* want you to be."

Well-being is subjective and highly personal; what works to increase one's happiness fails for another. So how do we measure it? The next section explores how individuals can take ownership of measuring their own success, using well-being as the primary metric.

THE STORIES OF OUR LIVES

During performance review season at Google, my manager, Sandy, sat me down in a small, windowless conference room and told me how happy she was with my work. She said I was doing all the right things, and that she considered me one of the best on her team. Then, she tried letting me down gently: my promotion didn't go through. I'd been at Google for ten years at that point, and had tried and failed to get promoted over the last several quarters. Sandy had promised that this time around it was a done deal, and I'd sail through the promotions committee. So, the news that it didn't get approved came as a bit of a shock. My initial reaction was uncharacteristic anger, the kind I only feel when disrespected by people or a system I once trusted. I went on a short but intense rant, sharing my feelings about the unfairness of it all, when something dawned on me. If I *had* gotten the promotion, I would've had to stay on my current project for at least two more years. And at that point, I was already tired of it and itching for something new. The promotion would have locked me in, and I'd have had to build out a team, something that held no interest for me.

I paused mid-rant to silently contemplate the irony. Then I muttered a thought out loud: "I don't think I want a promotion." Sandy was confused but gave me a minute of space. I knew I deserved *something* for all of my effort, but if it wasn't a promotion, then what the hell *did* I want?

I continued, "Sandy, I put so much of myself into this job. For over a decade, all I've done is give and give and give to Google. And I don't really know what I'm getting in return."

"Marissa, I promise you will get it next cycle. We just need to be pa—"

I jumped in. "No, that's not it. It's dawning on me that I really don't know *what* I want in return."

"I assumed you wanted the promotion." She was just as confused as I was.

"I did too. But when I really think about it . . . The only thing I want more of is money, and I'm not sure the price of staying on this project is even worth it."

"That's really helpful for me to know," she said.

Yeah, for me too.

Insane as it might seem, it took almost eleven years for me to realize I was working hard for stuff I didn't want. Instead of figuring out what I wanted, then making it happen, I was going along with a script of how things were supposed to happen.

The fabric of human culture is woven from stories. They tell us what we should do, who we should be, what to expect, and what is expected from us. Some of these stories are useful toward building a civilized, productive society. For example, the classic rags-to-riches story gives hope to people who might otherwise see their circumstances as permanent. Other stories, such as "vaccines cause autism" are toxic, and some bring out the worst of our nature. Many are embraced as truths, and few are ever examined or questioned.

Many of the stories we live by are based on who *other* people think we should be or what we should be doing. In his book *How I Found Freedom in an Unfree World*, Harry Browne says that when we follow stories blindly, as I did in the case of my promotion, they become mental traps.[6] If you volunteer to be the class mom at your child's elementary school because that's what "good moms" do, and not because you find this activity meaningful as a parent, you're in a mental trap. If you pursue a promotion because doing so makes you a "good employee," and not because you genuinely need the money or want the added responsibility, you're in a trap.

Books like *Lean In* and *Nice Girls Don't Get the Corner Office* are also stories, ones that have become so embedded in our culture that we rarely stop to question them. Their narratives provide a loose set of instructions and guide decisions about our careers in ways we don't even realize.

To illustrate, let's say I'm a young woman just starting out in my career. I read *Lean In* for the first time and buy into it hook, line, and sinker. I believe that women are at a disadvantage due to cultural expectations, and that if I hadn't been conditioned by these forces, I'd be in the same jobs and reach the same heights as men. How might this narrative affect the way I think about my career and guide my decisions?

First of all, I would probably be a little angry and maybe even defensive. Why should success be harder for me because I'm a woman? It's not fair that I have to do more work for less reward. The frustration also fuels me. I'm determined to prove my worth, and I work hard to seize my rightful seat at the big-boy table. *I lean all the way in.* I go for *all* the promotions. Sometimes I notice a subtle ambivalence about my career and question whether this is what I'm supposed to be doing. I dismiss it. It's my socialization acting up. I need to be more assertive and focus on the win. When I hit setbacks, I view them as evidence of gender bias. I tell the women on my team to stop using emojis. I congratulate myself for being so supportive. I'm determined to succeed. I'm unhappy, but I don't know why. I accept that this is just the way it is.

How am I making career and life decisions in the above scenario? I'm not. I'm following a script.

In the 1950s, there were no overarching career narratives for women. The story dominating American women's lives at the time was about staying home and raising children. Most of us who have careers today would've been housewives in that era. Not because it was illegal for women to enter the workforce (it wasn't), but because that script dominated our culture, and we would've followed along. Whether we'd be happier as a modern career woman or a fifties housewife is irrelevant; a narrative would direct our lives all the same.

Living out a story isn't universally bad, and our tendency to do so isn't some indictment of human nature. We're not all blind, ignorant sheep, as I've accused many others of saying. It's not a gender thing, not a cultural oppression thing. Stories are incredibly valuable and uniquely human. We *need* stories to give our lives meaning and provide a structure to help us make sense of things. For instance, one thing that helped me survive my ordeal at Facebook was conceptualizing the experience as part of my own hero's journey. The hero's journey is a story template in which the main character goes through several phases of trials and tribulations and comes out the other side as a hero. It helped me see the difficulty as a necessary part of my life's journey, which I trusted would lead me to a better place. I was following a script, and I'm certain the arc led me to write this book and pursue my dreams. The difference between this narrative and the one I was living at Google is who wrote it.

Stories become troublesome only when we lose sight of which one we're living. When we don't write our own scripts, or when we fail to realize we're following someone else's, we're more likely to act against our best interests and sacrifice our happiness.

I'm not suggesting that women who aren't fulfilled in their careers should straight up quit and write a book. Or walk away altogether. I understand how unrealistic that is for most people. And this isn't a self-help book; I can't tell you what to do or what changes you need to make or what's going well for you. I'm simply reframing some of the stories we've been told in the hopes that we think more critically about the ones we live by. The good news is, while stories are a central force in our lives, we have the power to write our own. And the first step is trying to understand the main character.

DORIS

"We don't wipe our mouths with our underwear!"

Words I never thought I'd say in my lifetime. Until I had boys.

One night I was sitting at the kitchen table with my son, who was eight at the time. He was eating dinner in his underwear while zoned in to his favorite show on TV, and when some mac and cheese dribbled down his chin, I watched as he pulled his underwear up to his face and wiped it off. In case the image isn't 100 percent clear: he used his underwear as a napkin. While a pile of actual napkins sat only a few inches away on the table. I was part incredulous and part impressed. He was so into the show, he couldn't be bothered to make even the tiniest effort to use a real napkin.

In that moment, my son just did not give a f*ck.

As an avid consumer of personal development and productivity books, I couldn't help but see the act as both extraordinarily lazy and ingenuously efficient. It reminded me of the current cultural lexicon in self-help, popularized by author Mark Manson in his book *The Subtle Art of Not Giving a F*ck* (HarperCollins, 2016). The concept is simple: we only have so many f*cks to give in life, so make sure you're only giving them to the worthiest things. In the case of my son, his allocation of f*cks didn't extend to hygiene or social decorum.

God love him.

My knee-jerk reaction was judgment and mild disgust. But he was going to shower and throw his clothes in the laundry right after dinner. Would it do any lasting damage? Would the underwear-as-napkin incident be a gateway drug to boxer-briefs-as-toilet-paper in ten years?

Perhaps my disgust was warranted in that moment, but it reminded me of all the times my lack of f*cks was similarly judged. As a single mom of three kids, managing a household solo, with a three-hour daily commute, and a demanding, full-time job, I'm often overwhelmed with homework, activities, playdates, sports, and the pesky responsibilities of having to feed, clothe, and spend time with my kids. As a matter of survival, there's a whole list of things I've had to stop caring about. To decide what goes on this list, I came up with a handy mental device, and her name is Doris.

In moments when I catch myself giving a f*ck about something that may or may not be worth the energy, I conjure an image of myself at eighty years old. For some reason I call her "Doris," and she's always sitting on a porch in a muumuu, drinking scotch. I imagine what Doris would say to me about the situation at hand. Most of the time, she's muttering in a raspy voice and telling me in one way or another to chill the hell out. I called upon Doris shortly after my son wiped his face with his underwear.

Removing a joint from her lips and setting her glass of scotch on the table, Doris delivered a rambling, semicoherent pearl of wisdom:

"Life is messy, and sometimes ya gotta just put on your big-girl panties and deal with it. If it means you need to use those panties to wipe up some mac and cheese from your face every once in a while, so be it."

God love her.

Doris is more than a way to justify the messiness in my life. She offers a distance and perspective that help me see what matters at the end of it all. And she reminds me that much of my stress comes from external pressure, not anything real. She's a reminder that at the end of it all, the most important thing is to be true to myself.

What Doris really represents is my well-being.

While Doris works great for *me*, I'm not suggesting that the cure for career dissatisfaction is an eighty-year-old alcoholic in a muumuu. Other, more concrete ways exist to organize your career around well-being. During my workshops at Google, I used a needs-assessment exercise to get people thinking about some critical elements of their well-being, which were meant as building blocks on their journey toward fulfillment.

To set expectations, it's not a one-two-three list of things to do for a rewarding career. There are already so many books filled with prescriptive career advice. I found happiness and fulfillment by leaning out of corporate America. You may find it by leaning in. Regardless of your particular ambition, the journey toward a meaningful life and career must start by looking within. This is just one example of something you can use to keep you honest about what's driving your choices and which story you're following.

As an aside, I understand the irony of telling you how to be happy by railing against others who tell you how to be happy. The only thing I can say is that you also have to choose which stories to believe. If mine doesn't work for your life, by all means, ignore it. The other irony is, if you do ignore it, you'll still be following my advice!

———————

As you may remember from school, Abraham Maslow's hierarchy of needs tells us that once human beings fulfill their basic survival needs (food, clothing, shelter), the most significant force driving behavior is our emotional needs. Different categories make up our emotional needs, all with different names and labels, but the ones I've found most helpful and taught in my workshops are *security, power, freedom, and connection.*

How high or low our needs are in each category is what makes each person unique and is a large part of our personalities. For example, I have a high need for freedom and a low need for power. This explains a lot about why I never fit well in corporate America, by the way. Because of my high need for freedom, flexibility was a central piece of my fulfillment. By flexibility, I don't just mean the ability to work from home, although that's part of it. It also means I needed the flexibility to work *how* I work best. Nobody likes a micromanager, but as a creative person, my brain can't function in the linear way that many managers required of me. I was always more successful when I was managed by people who trusted me to work independently and were comfortable with the fact that I drew outside the lines.

A large part of our happiness and well-being is determined by how we're meeting and fulfilling our emotional needs. That's why it's important to understand where we fall on the spectrum in each category; without an intimate understanding of our needs, it's difficult to fulfill them. These categories aren't meant to be clinical definitions.

You'll find a wide variety with similar themes across the social sciences. However, what they lack in precision they make up for in simplicity and practicality. They provide a starting point to better understand your individual needs and desires.

Here's an overview of each need:

- **Security:** The need for security describes the extent to which one needs structure, order, and both financial and job security. People with a high need for security want to know the rules and exactly what's expected of them, and prefer that things are done by the book. They do well in highly structured environments where there's order, and when they have a clear sense of duty and purpose within that structure.

- **Power:** In this context, power means the need for control, not power to affect the world at large. Those who score high on the need for power are achievement oriented and competitive. At work, their emotional needs are status, prestige, and respect. Because they derive satisfaction from control, they're more comfortable in positions of management and authority.

- **Freedom:** People with a high need for freedom are extremely uncomfortable being told what they can and can't do. They appreciate independence and the opportunity to express themselves freely. Many creative people fall into this category. At work, their emotional needs are met by being well-liked and approved of, and by having fun.

- **Connection:** People who have a high need for connection derive much of their satisfaction from relationships. They are most comfortable helping others and in environments based on trust and cooperation. Their emotional needs at work include being accepted, being liked, and maintaining harmony among coworkers.

You can learn more about your emotional needs and personality type in various ways. The four needs listed above are a small subset of much broader and more extensive ones; they were simply the labels I found most useful. However you slice it, it's critical that you develop a better sense of who you are and what you need. The exact method you choose or framework you pick is irrelevant.

With that said, the first step is to plot where you fall along the spectrum of needs in each category. Here is a list of statements that will help you figure out which of your emotional needs are stronger:

- Security
  - I like it when things are done by the book.
  - I like being prepared in advance and knowing what's expected of me.
  - I like being precise and staying organized.
  - To convince me of something, I need cold, hard facts.
  - I fear disorder and confusion.
- Power
  - I value respect over admiration.
  - I am very comfortable asserting my needs and wants.
  - I thrive in competition.
  - I am decisive and self-reliant.
  - I fear failure and losing control.
- Freedom
  - I need room to be spontaneous.
  - Flexibility in my schedule and workspace is important to me.
  - At work, I'd rather go with the flow than follow a rigid plan.
  - I'm uncomfortable in environments with a rigid structure where everything is done by the book.
  - I fear being restrained or controlled.

- Connection
  - I'd rather be well-liked than well respected.
  - I'm better at accommodating other people's needs than asserting my own.
  - I fear rejection and conflict.

The areas where you have the highest needs are the most important to pay attention to, because satisfying them is critical to your well-being. Once you understand your level of need in each category, it can become a sort of compass for well-being and a guide to decision-making in your career. For example, if you have a low need for power but a high need for security, you're probably better off negotiating for a raise than for the spot of team manager. If you have a high need for power and freedom, running your own business would be a great long-term goal.

If you recognize that your needs aren't being met, it doesn't mean you need to change jobs or companies or even what you're doing every day. Going through these exercises, I realized that my needs weren't being met at work, but it took years before I figured out how to change it. Most important, it helped me recognize that nobody was going to fill my needs for me. I couldn't rely on the institution of Google, or Facebook, or anyone really, to know what I needed and wanted and to give it to me when it was deserved. Real empowerment is about knowing who you are and how to fulfill your unique needs and desires. The above exercise is just one example of how to take ownership of your well-being and reframe your career around personal fulfillment.

———

My performance review meeting with Sandy was the first time I asked for what I truly wanted in return for my years of hard work. I believe that one small truth sparked a more lasting pattern of self-honesty that, after many years, led to me writing this book. And it began with one question: What do I want? It was the first moment I turned around and asked myself what I needed and wanted instead of accepting whatever the system spit out as a reward.

Two weeks after our conversation about the promotion, I was sitting at my desk when I saw an email from Sandy's manager pop up in my in-box. In it, he thanked me for my contributions to Google and said they were going to use 60 percent of their discretionary budget to award me a spot bonus. It was a large sum of money that I wasn't expecting. I was floored. I had asked for what I wanted, and I got it. Had I remained stuck in the false notion that I needed and wanted a promotion, I would've received neither the promotion *nor* the money. But to get what I wanted, I first had to know what it was. In that moment it was money, but as time went on, and I got more honest with myself about who I am and what I wanted, the process grew into a much bigger journey toward fulfillment.

Lean out doesn't mean quit your job or check out mentally. It means leaning out of anyone else's story of who you should be and what a successful career looks like. It's a rejection of dogma and rhetoric. It's about declining the invitation to model your career after people you don't want to become. But it also doesn't mean that if your job is less than ideal, the situation is hopeless. It's just a recognition that our institutions, as they're designed today, aren't equipped to fulfill everyone's needs. Our systems must evolve, and until they do, they're leaving a treasure of diverse talent on the table. But things won't change overnight, and in the meantime, it's up to us to recognize the limitations of the system in which we work, and understand that it cannot always fulfill our deepest human needs and acknowledge the depth of our contribution. When we recognize that we're looking for satisfaction in all the wrong places, the pain of our jobs begins to release its grip, and we can find alternative ways to fulfill our needs.

ACKNOWLEDGMENTS

When a single mom of three has a lucrative career at the best companies in the world, and then decides to forgo all of it in pursuit of writing a book, something for which she has neither experience nor credentials, it's easy to dismiss the whole thing as a crazy fantasy that's not worth the risk. So I'd like to start by thanking all the people who believed in me and encouraged me to continue hustling toward my dream.

Eric, from the moment I mentioned my plan to write a book in the summer of 2016, you treated it as if success was a foregone conclusion. For that, I am eternally grateful. Thank you for being my rock and my best friend. I love you so much.

Sara, you are a sister to me. Thank you for being there at every step of the journey and injecting much needed laughter into the daily slog of writing. Friendships like ours are what makes my life worth living.

To Sherika, my sister-wife, thank you for being there all those times I'd call you freaking out over a deadline or a last round of edits I needed to make, and for dropping everything to come over and be with the kids. You are a member of our family, and you make our lives better, more fulfilled, and of course, way more fun. This book could not have been written without you.

To Carol, who not only let me make fun of her in this book, but also reveled in it. Thank you for being a constant in my life and for supporting me all the way through.

Donna, I'll never forget your reaction when I first told you I was going to write a book. Without pausing, you said, "It's about time." Thank you for believing in me and for devoting your free time to create graphics for my original book proposal.

Julie, I hope you'll never look at a fishbowl conference room the same way again. Thank you for listening to me hash out my ideas and outlines in the earliest stages of this project.

Will, what would I have done without my work-from-home husband? Sitting at my living-room desk, writing for all those long days, weeks, months . . . I felt like Jack Nicholson in *The Shining*. Thank you for our therapy and gossip sessions, which got me through it all without going completely mental.

Jodi, thank you for taking time to read my early drafts, giving me such helpful feedback, and for letting me put our college memories out there for the world to enjoy.

Jeff, thank you for being so understanding and flexible with our schedules. I really appreciate the relationship and communication we've cultivated over the past several years and am deeply grateful for your support.

Michael, like the kid in *The Sixth Sense* who saw dead people, you saw something in me during a time I felt the most invisible. I will never ever forget that.

Greg, thank you for being more than just an agent—you're also a great partner and friend. From day one, you just "got it." You believed in me and my message and have been a tireless champion of moving it forward.

To my most amazing team at HarperCollins Leadership. You guys have made this whole experience so much better and more fun, and I am deeply grateful for having had the chance to work with such a stellar group.

Jeff, thank you for taking a chance on me. I can only imagine how hard you had to work to sell it in and make it happen, and ever since, you've worked tirelessly to support it at every step of the way.

To my fabulous pair of editors, Tim and Amanda, you helped turn coal into diamonds. Tim, thank you for helping me take a messy first draft and turn it into something I could be really proud of. Amanda, thank you for your enthusiasm, friendship, and the hours of work you put in over weekends and late nights at home to meet our tight deadlines. This book would not be what it is without you.

Sicily, when I think of people who "lead from behind," you are one of the first who comes to mind. You moved this project forward in so many ways, big and small; thank you for being such a great partner.

To Hiram, one of my most enthusiastic supporters, thank you for lending all your hard work and expertise toward getting my message out into the world.

To Tracy at Rogers and Cowan, thank you for all your hard work on launching this book into the market and gaining the right people's attention.

To Tucker, Hal, Mark, Emily, Charlie, and the whole team at Scribe—what I learned from you guys in Austin was perhaps the most critical turning point in my ability to write this book. I went from writing in circles to writing something that actually resembled a first draft. I can't thank you enough for the insights, support, and encouragement.

And finally, to my A-team: Zachary, Jake, and Shelby. You guys are the light of my life, my heart, my soul, and my purpose. I love you to the ends of the earth, just the way you are.

NOTES

INTRODUCTION

1. Jeff Moss, "Emotional Intelligence in Business and Leadership," *Forbes*, November 13, 2018, https://www.forbes.com/sites/forbesnycouncil /2018/11/13/emotional-intelligence-in-business-and-leadership /#f75283659eb5.

2. See, for example, Maryam Meshkat and Reza Nejati, "Does Emotional Intelligence Depend on Gender? A Study on Undergraduate English Majors of Three Iranian Universities," SAGE Open, August 30, 2017, https://doi.org/10.1177/2158244017725796; and Daily Mail, "Women Are Better Listeners, Study Says," *Gulf News Europe*, February 13, 2014, https://gulfnews.com/world/europe/women-are-better-listeners-study -says-1.1290574.

CHAPTER 1: SILENCING THE LAMBS

1. People who've never worked in the corporate world are often shocked to find out that doing work isn't required to be successful.

2. Curiously, this only applied to people in the business organization; engineers didn't have the same policy.

3. Tony Robbins, *Awaken the Giant Within: How to Take Immediate Control of Your Mental, Emotional, Physical and Financial Destiny!* (New York: Simon & Schuster, 2007), 89.

4. Sheryl Sandberg, *Lean In: Women, Work, and the Will to Lead* (New York: Knopf, 2013), 21.

5. Zameena Mejia, "Just 24 Female CEOs Lead the Companies on the 2018 Fortune 500—Fewer Than Last Year," CNBC, May 21, 2018,

https://www.cnbc.com/2018/05/21/2018s-fortune-500-companies-have
-just-24-female-ceos.html.

6. Kevin Miller and Deborah J. Vagins, "The Simple Truth about the
Gender Pay Gap," American Association of University Women, 2018,
https://www.aauw.org/research/the-simple-truth-about-the-gender
-pay-gap/.

CHAPTER 2: FREE TO BE JUST LIKE ME

1. Sheryl Sandberg, "An equal world will be one where women run half
our countries and companies and men run half our homes," Facebook,
March 6, 2018, https://www.facebook.com/sheryl/posts/10159982519
515177.

2. Judith Ronin, quoted in Sandberg, *Lean In*, 14 (see chap. 1, n. 4).

3. Lareina Yee et al., *Women in the Workplace 2016*, a joint study by
LeanIn.org and McKinsey & Company, https://30percentclub.org
/assets/uploads/Ireland/PDFs/Women_in_the_Workplace_2016.pdf, 15.

4. Sandberg, *Lean In*, 15.

5. Sandberg, 19.

6. Sandberg, 40.

7. Sandberg, 12.

8. Sandberg, 24.

9. Sandberg, 24–25.

10. Sandberg, 24.

11. "Number and Percentage Distribution of Teachers in Public and Private
Elementary and Secondary Schools, by Selected Teacher Characteristics:
Selected Years, 1987–88 through 2015–16," *Digest of Education Statistics*,
2017, https://nces.ed.gov/programs/digest/d17/tables/dt17_209.10.asp
?current=yes.

12. Yee et al., *Women in the Workplace 2016*, 16.

13. Yee et al., 16.

14. Chloe Tejada, "Women Still Do More Chores at Home Than Men, Study
Finds," *HuffPost*, updated October 19, 2018, https://www.huffingtonpost
.ca/2017/09/27/women-chores-home_a_23224733/; and "Household
Chores: Women Still Do More," Springer, September 26, 2017, https://www
.springer.com/gp/about-springer/media/research-news/all-english
-research-news/household-chores--women-still-do-more-/15086994.

15. Edward Podolsky, *Sex Today in Wedded Life* (New York: Simon Publications, 1947), 236–37.

16. See, for example, Lois P. Frankel, *Nice Girls Don't Get the Corner Office: 101 Unconscious Mistakes Women Make That Sabotage Their Careers* (New York: Hachette, 2004), "Just say no to feeding people at work" (mistake 27).

CHAPTER 3: THE CONFIDENCE GAP

1. Joyce Ehrlinger and David Dunning, "How Chronic Self-Views Influence (and Potentially Mislead) Estimates of Performance," *Journal of Personality and Social Psychology* 84, no. 1 (2003): 5–17, http://doi.org/10.1037/0022-3514.84.1.5.

2. Ehrlinger and Dunning, "Chronic Self-Views," 11.

3. Katty Kay and Claire Shipman, "The Confidence Gap," *Atlantic*, May 2014, https://www.theatlantic.com/magazine/archive/2014/05/the-confidence-gap/359815/.

4. I had to google that last word. It means "acting in an evasive way that borders on lying." Katty Kay and Claire Shipman, *The Confidence Code: The Science and Art of Self-Assurance—What Women Should Know* (2014; repr., New York: HarperBusiness, 2018), xxvi.

5. Kay and Shipman, *The Confidence Code*, xxi.

6. Kay and Shipman, xxv.

7. Glenn Croston, "The Thing We Fear More Than Death," *Psychology Today*, November 29, 2012, https://www.psychologytoday.com/us/blog/the-real-story-risk/201211/the-thing-we-fear-more-death.

8. Kay and Shipman, *The Confidence Code*, 50.

9. Kay and Shipman, 19–20.

10. Kay and Shipman, 19.

11. Kay and Shipman, 36–37.

12. Nathaniel Branden, *The Six Pillars of Self-Esteem* (New York: Bantam, 1995), 4.

13. Branden, *Six Pillars of Self-Esteem*, 40, 43, 77.

14. Branden, 5–6.

15. Yee et al., *Women in the Workplace 2016*, 15 (see chap. 2, n. 3).

16. Linda Babcock and Sara Laschever, *Women Don't Ask: The High Cost of Avoiding Negotiation—and Positive Strategies for Change* (New York: Bantam, 2007), 1–2.

17. Babcock and Laschever, *Women Don't Ask*, 5.
18. Chris Voss, with Tahl Raz, *Never Split the Difference: Negotiating As If Your Life Depended on It* (New York: HarperBusiness, 2016), 192.
19. Voss, *Never Split the Difference*, 193.
20. Tel Aviv University, "Study Finds Women Achieve Better Results When Negotiating on Behalf of Friends," Phys.org, September 7, 2016, https://phys.org/news/2016-09-women-results-behalf-friends.html#jCp.
21. Jens Mazei et al., "A Meta-Analysis on Gender Differences in Negotiation Outcomes and Their Moderators," *Psychological Bulletin* 141, no. 1 (2015): 85–104, https://www.apa.org/pubs/journals/releases/bul-a0038184.pdf.
22. Danielle Pacquette, "Men Can't Compromise Without Women Around," *Washington Post*, August 2, 2016, https://www.washingtonpost.com/news/wonk/wp/2016/08/02/men-cant-compromise-without-women-around/?utm_term=.4bcd425f841a.

CHAPTER 4: PUTTING THE *MEN* IN *MENTOR*

1. See "Why Mentorship Matters," LeanIn.org, https://leanin.org/mentor-her.
2. "Finding a Guide: The Value of Having a Professional Mentor," Common Good Careers, Knowledge Center, accessed January 30, 2019, http://commongoodcareers.org/articles/detail/finding-a-guide-the-value-of-having-a-professional-mentor.
3. Melissa Healy, "Science Confirms That Women Reap Health Benefits from Friendships," *Seattle Times*, June 15, 2005, https://www.seattletimes.com/seattle-news/health/science-confirms-that-women-reap-health-benefits-from-friendships/.
4. Alice Robb, "Authors of Romance Novels Are Big Sellers, but Still Deal with an Age-Old Stigma," Women in the World, July 20, 2015, https://womenintheworld.com/2015/07/20/a-peek-at-the-authors-who-write-romance-novels-and-the-stigmas-they-experience/.
5. Laurie Kahn, "10 Surprising Facts About Romance Novels," *The Blog, HuffPost,* updated June 22, 2015, https://www.huffingtonpost.ca/laurie-kahn/romance-novels_b_7109458.html.
6. Ann Gibbons, "Bonobos Join Chimps as Closest Human Relatives," *Science*, June 13, 2012, https://www.sciencemag.org/news/2012/06/bonobos-join-chimps-closest-human-relatives.

7. Kristina Cawthon Lang, "Bonobo: *Pan paniscus*," Primate Info Net, last modified December 1, 2010, http://pin.primate.wisc.edu/factsheets /entry/bonobo/behav.

8. Angela Saini, "Scientists Assumed That Patriarchy Was Only Natural. Bonobos Proved Them Wrong," *Monkey Business* (a Quartz blog), July 20, 2017, https://qz.com/1033621/scientists-assumed-that-patriarchy -was-only-natural-bonobos-proved-them-wrong/.

9. Saini, "Scientists Assumed."

10. Kristen Fuller, "The Importance of Female Friendships Among Women," *Psychology Today*, August 16, 2018, https://www.psychology today.com/us/blog/happiness-is-state-mind/201808/the-importance -female-friendships-among-women.

11. Samantha Olson, "Women Work Well in Groups Unless There's Competition; Men Are Complete Opposite," *Medical Daily*, August 13, 2014, https://www.medicaldaily.com/women-work-well-groups-unless -theres-competition-men-are-complete-opposite-297992.

CHAPTER 5: SCHOOL VS. WORK

1. Anne Stych, "Women Earn the Majority of Advanced Degrees," *Bizwomen*, October 9, 2018, https://www.bizjournals.com/bizwomen /news/latest-news/2018/10/women-earn-the-majority-of-advanced -degrees.html.

2. Frankel, *Nice Girls Don't Get the Corner Office*, 2 (see chap. 2, n. 16).

3. Babcock and Laschever, *Women Don't Ask*, 74 (see chap. 3, n. 16).

4. Kay and Shipman, *The Confidence Code*, 87–88 (see chap. 3, n. 4).

5. Kay and Shipman, 88.

6. Curt Rice, "How Blind Auditions Help Orchestras to Eliminate Gender Bias," *The Guardian*, October 13, 2013, https://www.theguardian.com /women-in-leadership/2013/oct/14/blind-auditions-orchestras-gender-bias.

CHAPTER 6: #SORRYNOTSORRY

1. Babcock and Laschever, *Women Don't Ask*, 8 (see chap. 3, n. 16).

2. Babcock and Laschever, 14.

3. Babcock and Laschever, ix.

4. Babcock and Laschever, 2.

5. Babcock and Laschever, 2.

6. Rachel Thomas et al., *Women in the Workplace 2017*, a joint study by LeanIn.org and McKinsey & Company, https://womenintheworkplace.com/2017, 10.

7. Thomas et al., *Women in the Workplace 2017*, 10, emphasis added.

8. Frankel, *Nice Girls Still Don't Get the Corner Office: Unconscious Mistakes Women Make That Sabotage Their Careers* (New York; Boston: Business Plus, 2014), xviii–xix.

9. Frankel, *Nice Girls Still Don't Get*, xxiii.

10. Frankel, 1.

11. Frankel, 4.

12. Frankel, 20.

13. Frankel, 20.

14. Frankel, 20–21.

15. Frankel, 20.

16. Frankel, 20.

17. See Frankel, ix-xiv, "Contents," for the full list.

18. Frankel, 47.

19. Frankel, 56.

20. Frankel, 112.

21. Frankel, 112.

22. Sandberg, *Lean In*, 39–40 (see chap. 1, n. 4).

23. The Notorious B.I.G., "Playa Hater," by Notorious B.I.G., Daddy's House Recording Studios, 1997.

24. Shana Lebowitz, "The 'Big 5' Personality Traits Could Predict Who Will and Won't Become a Leader," *Business Insider*, December 7, 2016, https://www.businessinsider.com/big-five-personality-traits-predict-leadership-2016-12.

25. Lebowitz, "The 'Big 5' Personality Traits."

26. Shana Lebowitz, "Why People with Agreeable Personalities Are Less Likely to Become Top Managers," *Business Insider*, May 7, 2015, https://www.businessinsider.com/agreeable-personality-and-leadership-2015-5.

27. Timothy A. Judge, Beth A. Livingston, and Charlice Hurst, "Do Nice Guys—and Gals—Really Finish Last? The Joint Effects of Sex and Agreeableness on Income," *Journal of Personality and Social Psychology* 102, no. 2 (February 2012): 390–407, https://doi.org/10.1037/a002602.

28. Thomas W. H. Ng et al., "Predictors of Objective and Subjective Career

Success: A Meta-Analysis," *Personnel Psychology* 58, no. 2 (June 2005): 367–408, https://doi.org/10.1111/j.1744-6570.2005.00515.x; Gerrit Mueller and Erik J. S. Plug, "Estimating the Effect of Personality on Male and Female Earnings," *ILR Review* 60, no. 1 (2006): 3–22, https://doi.org/10.1177/001979390606000101; and Ellen K. Nyhus and Empar Pons, "The Effects of Personality on Earnings," *Journal of Economic Psychology* 26, no. 3 (June 2005): 363–84, https://doi.org/10.1016/j.joep .2004.07.001.

CHAPTER 7: THE POWER REWARD

1. Power over oneself is a subset of the global definition, as it can serve as protection from external pressure or influence, and produce feelings such as respect.
2. Agency, "Female Bosses Who Can Hire and Fire More Likely to Suffer Depression," *Telegraph*, November 19, 2014, https://www.telegraph.co .uk/finance/jobs/11240453/Female-bosses-who-can-hire-and-fire-more -likely-to-suffer-depression.html.
3. Francesca Gino, Caroline Ashley Wilmuth, and Alison Wood Brooks, "Compared to Men, Women View Professional Advancement as Equally Attainable, but Less Desirable," *Proceedings of the National Academy of Sciences of the United States of America* 112, no. 40 (October 6, 2015), https://doi.org/10.1073/pnas.1502567112.
4. Mark Koba, "Women in Power: Yes, They Are Different from Men," CNBC, October 10, 2011, https://www.cnbc.com/id/44687913.
5. Anna Muoio, "Women and Men, Work and Power," *Fast Company*, January 31, 1998, https://www.fastcompany.com/33732/women-and -men-work-and-power.
6. Carmen Nobel, "Men Want Powerful Jobs More Than Women Do," *Working Knowledge* (a Harvard Business School blog), September 23, 2015, https://hbswk.hbs.edu/item/men-want-powerful-jobs-more -than-women-do.
7. Katherine A. Cronin et al., "Hierarchy Is Detrimental for Human Cooperation," *Science Reports* 5, art. no. 18634 (December 22, 2015), https://www.nature.com/articles/srep18634.
8. Frankel, *Nice Girls Still Don't Get the Corner Office*, 20 (see chap. 6, n. 8).
9. Babcock and Laschever, *Women Don't Ask*, ix–x (see chap. 3, n. 16).

CHAPTER 8: IT'S THE SYSTEM, STUPID!

1. Michael Lewis, *Moneyball: The Art of Winning an Unfair Game* (New York: W. W. Norton, 2004), 18.

2. Michael Lewis, *The Undoing Project: A Friendship That Changed Our Minds* (New York: W. W. Norton, 2017).

3. Khalil Smith, "Why Our Brains Fall for False Expertise, and How to Stop It," *Strategy+Business*, March 5, 2018, https://www.strategy -business.com/article/Why-Our-Brains-Fall-for-False-Expertise -and-How-to-Stop-It.

4. Gert Stulp et al., "Human Height Is Positively Related to Interpersonal Dominance in Dyadic Interactions," *PLoS One* 10, no. 2 (February 26, 2015), https://www.ncbi.nlm.nih.gov/pmc/articles/PMC4342156/; and Sean Nealon, "Wide-Faced Men Negotiate Nearly $2,200 Larger Signing Bonus," Medical Press, July 23, 2014, https://medicalxpress.com/news /2014-07-wide-faced-men-larger-bonus.html.

5. Nancy M. Blaker et al., "The Height Leadership Advantage in Men and Women: Testing Evolutionary Psychology Predictions About the Perceptions of Tall Leaders," *Group Processes and Intergroup Relations* 16, no. 1 (2013): 17–27, https://doi.org/10.1177/1368430212437211.

6. Malcolm Gladwell, *Blink: The Power of Thinking Without Thinking* (New York: Little, Brown, 2005), 87.

7. Michael P. Haselhuhn et al., "Negotiating Face-to-Face: Men's Facial Structure Predicts Negotiation Performance," *Leadership Quarterly* 25, no. 5 (October 2014): 835–84, https://doi.org/10.1016/j.leaqua.2013 .12.003.

8. Nassim Nicholas Taleb, *The Black Swan: The Impact of the Highly Improbable*, 2nd ed. (New York: Random House, 2010), 132.

9. Bryce Nelson, "Aggression: Still a Stronger Trait for Males," *New York Times*, June 20, 1983, https://www.nytimes.com/1983/06/20/style /aggression-still-a-stronger-trait-for-males.html; Patrick Ring et al., "Gender Differences in Performance Predictions: Evidence from the Cognitive Reflection Test," *Frontiers in Psychology* 7 (2016), https:// www.ncbi.nlm.nih.gov/pmc/articles/PMC5089055/; and Susan E. Cross and Laura Madson, "Models of the Self: Self-Construals and Gender," *Psychological Bulletin* 122, no. 1 (1997): 5–37, https://doi.org/10.1037 /0033-2909.122.1.5.

10. Ashraf Labib and Martin Read, "Not Just Rearranging the Deckchairs on the *Titanic*: Learning from Failures through Risk and Reliability Analysis," *Safety Science* 51, no. 1 (2013): 397–413, https://doi.org/10.1016/j.ssci.2012.08.014; and Don Moore and Samuel A. Swift, "The Three Faces of Overconfidence in Organizations," in *Social Psychology and Organizations*, ed. David De Cremer, Rolf van Dick, and J. Keith Murnighan (New York and East Sussex: Routledge, 2010), 147–84.

11. Elizabeth Harris, "Q&A: Michael Lewis on Revisiting *Moneyball*, Male Overconfidence and the Future of Finance," *Forbes*, January 24, 2017, https://www.forbes.com/sites/elizabethharris/2017/01/24/qa-michael-lewis-on-revisiting-moneyball-male-overconfidence-and-the-future-of-finance/#344dd9aa698d.

12. Jeff Sommer, "How Men's Overconfidence Hurts Them as Investors," *New York Times*, March 13, 2010, https://www.nytimes.com/2010/03/14/business/14mark.html.

13. Sommer, "Men's Overconfidence."

14. Dan Ariely, "Are We in Control of Our Own Decisions?" TED video, December 2008, https://www.ted.com/talks/dan_ariely_asks_are_we_in_control_of_our_own_decisions?language=en.

15. Chip Heath and Dan Heath, *Switch: How to Change Things When Change Is Hard* (New York: Crown Business, 2010), 3.

16. Heath and Heath, *Switch*, 1–3.

17. "National Obesity Rates & Trends," State of Obesity (website), accessed January 31, 2019, https://stateofobesity.org/obesity-rates-trends-overview/.

18. Emily Stewart, "Women Are Running for Office in Record Numbers. In Corporate America, They're Losing Ground," Vox, June 8, 2018, https://www.vox.com/policy-and-politics/2018/6/8/17413254/women-fortune-500-ceos-politics-blue-wave.

CHAPTER 9: A NEW WAY FORWARD

1. Robert Greene, *The 48 Laws of Power* (New York: Penguin, 2000). See the contents pages for the list of all forty-eight laws.

2. Adapted from Julia Rozovsky, "The Five Keys to a Successful Google Team," *re:Work* (Google blog), November 17, 2015, https://rework.with google.com/blog/five-keys-to-a-successful-google-team/.

3. Rozozsky, "Five Keys."

4. Tae Kim, "Ray Dalio Made $50 Billion for His Clients, Topping List of Biggest Hedge Fund Moneymakers Ever," CNBC, January 26, 2018, https://www.cnbc.com/2018/01/26/ray-dalio-made-50-billion-for-his -clients-topping-list-of-biggest-hedge-fund-money-makers-ever.html.

5. Ray Dalio, "How to Build a Company Where the Best Ideas Win," TED video, April 2017, https://www.ted.com/talks/ray_dalio_how_to _build_a_company_where_the_best_ideas_win?language=en.

6. More information and resources on Bridgewater's tools, including Dot Collector, are included in the appendix of his book *Principles*, so I won't go into detail on how they work from a technical perspective. See Ray Dalio, *Principles* (New York: Simon & Schuster, 2010), 545–52.

7. Dalio, "How to Build a Company."

8. Dalio, *Principles*, 531.

9. Chip Heath and Dan Heath, *Decisive: How to Make Better Choices in Life and Work* (New York: Crown Business, 2013), 36.

10. Heath and Heath, *Decisive*, 36; emphasis in original.

11. Harry Browne, *How I Found Freedom in an Unfree World: A Handbook for Personal Liberty* (New York: Macmillan, 1973), 68.

12. O. C. Tanner, "The Business Case for Recognition: The Latest Research, Compelling Insights, and the Benefits of Effective Recognition," 2015, https://www.octanner.com/content/dam/oc-tanner/documents/white -papers/OCT15_the-business-case-for-recognition-white-paper.pdf.

13. Josh Bersin, "New Research Unlocks the Secret of Employee Recognition," *Forbes*, June 13, 2012, https://www.forbes.com/sites /joshbersin/2012/06/13/new-research-unlocks-the-secret-of-employee -recognition/#789add845276.

14. Rob Danna, "Recognition in the Workplace: It's Not What You Think It Is," *Forbes*, February 28, 2018, https://www.forbes.com/sites /forbescommunicationscouncil/2018/02/28/recognition-in-the -workplace-its-not-what-you-think-it-is/#1bcc87633da5.

15. Annamarie Mann and Nate Dvorak, "Employee Recognition: Low Cost, High Impact," Gallup, June 28, 2016, https://www.gallup.com /workplace/236441/employee-recognition-low-cost-high-impact.aspx.

16. Victor Lipman, "The Most Important Work Relationship to Work On," *Forbes*, July 1, 2017, https://www.forbes.com/sites/victorlipman/2017/07/01 /the-most-important-work-relationship-to-work-on/#7ac35c033412.

17. Richard Feloni, "Google's HR Boss Says the Best Managers Practice These 9 Habits," *Business Insider*, April 23, 2015, https://www.business insider.com/google-on-habits-of-best-managers-2015-4.

18. Steve Crabtree, "Worldwide, 13% of Employees Are Engaged at Work," Gallup, October 8, 2013, https://news.gallup.com/poll/165269/worldwide -employees-engaged-work.aspx.

19. Richard Feynman, *"Surely You're Joking, Mr. Feynman!": Adventures of a Curious Character* (New York: W. W. Norton, 1997), 28.

20. Feynman, *"Surely You're Joking,"* 29.

21. Kelly Clay, "Amazon.com Goes Down, Loses $66,240 per Minute," *Forbes*, August 19, 2013, https://www.forbes.com/sites/kellyclay/2013/08 /19/amazon-com-goes-down-loses-66240-per-minute/#37330433495c.

22. John Schwartz and Matthew L. Wald, "Final Shuttle Report Cites 'Broken Safety Culture' at NASA," *New York Times*, August 26, 2003, https://www.nytimes.com/2003/08/26/national/final-shuttle-report -cites-broken-safety-culture-at-nasa.html.

23. Alan Boyle and the Associated Press, "Shuttle Report Blames NASA Culture," NBC News, August 26, 2003, http://www.nbcnews.com/id /3077541/ns/technology_and_science-space/t/shuttle-report-blames -nasa-culture/#.XFNxJFxKiUk.

CHAPTER 10: WELL-BEING VS. WINNING

1. Glenn Kessler, "President Obama's Persistent '77-Cent' Claim on the Wage Gap Gets a New Pinocchio Rating," *Washington Post*, April 9, 2014, https://www.washingtonpost.com/news/fact-checker/wp/2014 /04/09/president-obamas-persistent-77-cent-claim-on-the-wage-gap -gets-a-new-pinocchio-rating/?utm_term=.3c1b669f1311.

2. Ariane Hegewisch, "The Gender Wage Gap: 2017; Earnings Differences by Gender, Race, and Ethnicity," Institute for Women's Policy Research, September 13, 2018, https://iwpr.org/publications/gender-wage-gap-2017/.

3. "The State of the Gender Pay Gap 2018," PayScale.com, accessed January 31, 2019, https://www.payscale.com/data/gender-pay-gap.

4. Michelle King, "Want a Piece of the 18 Trillion Dollar Female Economy? Start with Gender Bias," *Forbes*, May 24, 2017, https://www .forbes.com/sites/michelleking/2017/05/24/want-a-piece-of-the-18 -trillion-dollar-female-economy-start-with-gender-bias/#470d14656123.

NOTES

5. Federal Reserve and Yankelovich Monitor & Greenfield figures, cited in "Statistics on the Purchasing Power of Women," Girlpower Marketing, accessed January 31, 2019, https://girlpowermarketing.com /statistics-purchasing-power-women/.
6. Harry Browne, *How I Found Freedom in an Unfree World*, 25th anniv. ed. (Amazon Digital, 2014), loc. 84, Kindle.

INDEX

INDEX

INDEX

ABOUT THE AUTHOR

Marissa Orr spent fifteen years working at today's top tech giants, Google and Facebook. She has conducted talks for over three thousand people in the United States, Europe, and Asia-Pacific, at companies including Google, Twitter, and American Express, at universities such as Pace University and New School, and at other venues. Originally from Miami, Orr received her master's degree in decision and information sciences from the University of Florida. She now lives in New Jersey, where she is known for being awful at karaoke and for wearing pajamas on the carpool line.